Merry Stigmas Productions in association with Ham & Cheese Ltd presents

TopGear
The Pantomime

Starring
TV's RICHARD HAMMOND
as Dick Hammondington

Starring
TV's JAMES MAY
as the Widow Pedantic

Starring
TV's JEREMY CLARKSON
as the Jeremy in the Lamp

Featuring
AMY WILLIAMS
as Skeleton Bob Cratchit

and
THE STIG
as Goldie-opposite-locks

Dunsfold Hippopotamusdrome, Surrey
15 December 2011 - 8 January 2012

WARNING: This production contains strobe lighting, uncontrolled fires and attempts at acting that some people may find offensive

A Top Gear Christmas

BOOKS

INSTRUCTIONS

Thank you for purchasing this copy of *A Top Gear Christmas*. We hope it will give you many hours of reading pleasure. Before using the book, please take time to read these instructions and follow them where necessary.

1. Before using the book, unscrew the retaining screws on all four corners and carefully cut the securing straps with a pair of scissors.

k. Insert four AA batteries into the battery compartment on the underside, making sure that they are the correct way round, as shown on the diagram inside the lid.

xi. Insert tab C into the slot on the base and press home until a click is heard. Repeat on the corresponding parts of the auxiliary unit.

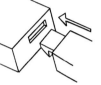

326. Ensure that lever F (marked with the radiator symbol) is in the down position before checking that each rissole is fully cooked using the hydraulic lifting system, remembering that this will only operate if all seven sensors detect no wolves have entered the main chamber and that the Ultra-bass™ function is set to zero using the red hand wheel on the right-hand side, taking care not to disturb the position of the principle measuring laser mounted on the upper right stanchion, which can also be used to remove stubborn stains from the work surfaces in the event that Mrs Wallingham is busy.

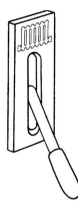

$. Gently fold the rest of the ingredients into the mixture and set to one side, then inflate the main chamber using the foot pump then press and hold the yellow button (marked G on your diagram) until a red light comes on. Wait for the red light to extinguish and turn the key once. If no humming sound is heard, wait for 15 seconds and then leave the house.

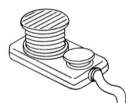

** Remember that pages 45–98 are NOT suitable for use in a microwave **

>. Breathe out.

A TOP GEAR CHRISTMAS

CONTENTS

Hello.

I was asked to write an
introduction to this book
but unfortunately there was a
programme about earthquakes
on the television at the time
and I literally couldn't
be bothered.

GETTING AROUND AT CHRISTMAS

TGV12 TRAIN

Speed:	High
Overtaking ability:	Risky
Windiness:	High
Noisiness:	Very high
Chance of ending up just outside Loughborough covered in excrement:	Almost certain

97cm approx

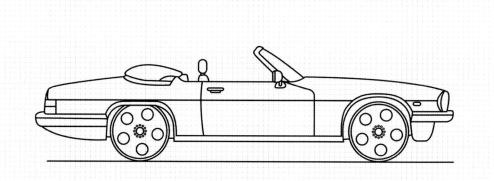

VW DAMPERVAN

Road speed:	Sluggish
Water speed:	Painful
Ability to make a cup of tea on board:	Reassuring
Ability to enter the water and sink immediately:	Worrying
Likely state of family's Christmas presents after journey:	Wet

212cm approx

Christmas time often involves travelling many miles to see friends and relatives, frequently risking delayed trains, cancelled flights and traffic congestion along the way. But there are alternative ways of getting around this Christmas thanks to the Top Gear Transport Solution System Solutions.

Here we outline the relative merits of our fleet.

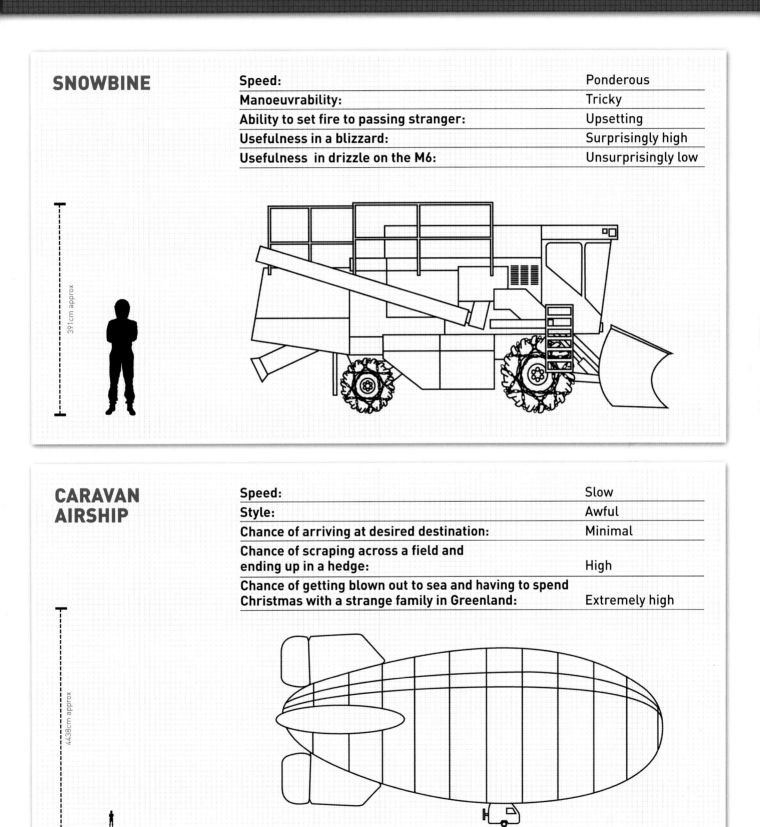

SNOWBINE

Speed:	Ponderous
Manoeuvrability:	Tricky
Ability to set fire to passing stranger:	Upsetting
Usefulness in a blizzard:	Surprisingly high
Usefulness in drizzle on the M6:	Unsurprisingly low

391cm approx

CARAVAN AIRSHIP

Speed:	Slow
Style:	Awful
Chance of arriving at desired destination:	Minimal
Chance of scraping across a field and ending up in a hedge:	High
Chance of getting blown out to sea and having to spend Christmas with a strange family in Greenland:	Extremely high

4438cm approx

IT'S NOT SNOW

IT'S STIG CAMOUFLAGE

CHRISTMAS SPEECH.

Hello. I am your supreme leader and unquestionable overlord of everything. Yes, that's right. I had a look at the constitutional monarchy small print and made some changes. As befits someone in my position, I am speaking to you today from an enormous black airship which is drifting slowly over Britain. As we know, Christmas is ideal for spending time with your family, unwrapping presents, eating lots of food and so on. For me, though, it is also a time for hovering menacingly over our great country and strafing things I don't like with a series of high-powered lasers. Indeed, you may at this very moment be wondering why the sky has gone black and there is an abnormal amount of screaming coming from your neighbour's house. Well, if you live in whatever town it is I'm over now and the house next door used to have some fake marble lions outside, all should now be clear. If I can get this stupid airship to stay still for two seconds, the 20-inch chrome wheels on your Range Rover Sport will be next.

Christmas is a time… stop drifting about you helium-filled idiot. Gah!

As I was saying, Christmas is a time for giving, and that is exactly why I will be giving that Peugeot dealership I passed over earlier a good solid dose of lead-based justice from my nose-mounted machine guns. Of course, Christmas is also a time for others to receive a selection of gifts. Although in my case, when I say 'others' I mean 'Bill Oddie' and when I say 'selection of gifts' I mean 'missile through his sitting room window'.

It goes without saying… Oh for God's sake, this isn't the right direction at all. Gnnnnrrrrr.

Where was I? Yes, it goes without saying that Christmas is a time of great joy, especially for those of us who have the capacity to hover behind Ed Miliband and hose him down with a 50 foot jet of flame, but it is also a time to reflect on those less fortunate than us such as Piers Morgan who, only yesterday, became crushed by a skip which fell from the sky in mysterious circumstances. I'm sure our sympathies would go out to his friends, if he had any.

At Christmas, we… What's it doing now?

No, no, no, this is all wrong, I want to go up…

For God's sake. Right… At Christmas we look forward to the future but we also look back to the past and reflect on the place where Birmingham used to be before it suffered an unexpected airbourne bombing campaign…

No, this is all wrong. WHY WON'T YOU STEER PROPERLY?

At this time of year we might also… JAMES! WHY IS IT DOING THIS? HAMMOND! IT'S DRIFTING TOWARDS SOME POWER LINES. Oh, wait. They're not there.

Yes, Christmas is a time to air regrets, and it is now that I regret having my two colleagues arrested, detained in the Tower of London and then beheaded.

Goodbye.

Silent Car

Silent car, electric car,
Not as fast as a Jaguar.
Rather small and slightly weird,
By the oil companies hardly feared,
You're as sexy as Vimto,
You're as sexy as mutton.

Silent car, electric car!
Sneaking up when we're unawar'
Full of jealousy, envy and hate
Mister Beardy in sandals your only mate.
You'd like to run everyone over
But that would take you til October

Silent car, electric car
Do you think you're going to go far?
You don't think it's particularly funny
That you'd be stuffed without a Duracell bunny.
You'd like to be a fierce raptor
But you can't go abroad without an adaptor.

THE HAMSTER'S SPEECH

At this time of year, it's very popular to just be very nasty about Christmas and how much you hate it. Well, if you don't like, don't do it! Be like all those people who used to take out adverts that said, 'Mr Alec Thompson will not be sending any Christmas cards this year.' Just don't buy any presents or have a turkey or answer the door to any carol singers. And they'll leave you alone. If you don't want to see it in the shops or on the telly, go away to Lundy and sit in a tent until January.

Or why not just enjoy it? It's Christmas, for goodness' sake. It only comes once a year and you get presents and food and Christmas specials and mistletoe. It's one day! And just to be completely cold-eyed and logical – let's compare the 25th of December to, say, February the 11th. Or October the 10th. Which is better? Are you telling me you'd really choose any other day of the year over Christmas?

Christmas is all right. Sometimes it's excellent. You see people you like. You might have to spend some time with relatives, but in the end, they're all cut from the same cloth as you. If they're a bit awful, then maybe you are too. And maybe they'd like to be spending Christmas on a sex boat in the Caribbean just as much as you would. Auntie Bessie was a bit of a goer back in the day.

Religious types can be very annoying, with their cardigans and their haircuts, but really, if all they want is for everyone to be a bit nicer to each other and remember the less fortunate and so on, they've got a fair point. After all, you've got 364 other days in the year to be a complete bastard to people if that's what you want.

So sit back in your cosy armchair, turn up the telly, pour yourself a possibly illegal measure of malt whisky, and – using this book as a shield – fall asleep in front of the fire. It's Christmas! It's like a week off with robins. Enjoy yourself!

Anyway, that's all I wanted to say, really. The rest is all song titles – have yourself a merry little etc. So it's goodnight from me and it's goodnight from him, and it's goodnight from him.

Merry Christmas, everybody!

Landlords Jeremy Clarkson & 'Captain' James May
reluctantly invite you to spend

Christmas at The FAT GUT

Now with fewer kitchen fires!

Christmas menu

STARTER
Crisps

MAIN
Shepherd's pie

Children must wear a tie. And not speak!

VEGETARIAN OPTION
Just eat the shepherd's pie or get out

PUDDING
Neither of us know how to do puddings.
Have some more shepherd's pie. With custard

Please remember that the following
conversational topics are banned:
*Golf, cricket, The Archers, the environment, MyFaceTwat,
business things, popular music after 1983, Milibands*

A WARM WELCOME IS FAIRLY UNLIKELY!

THE FAT GUT, SODDING COCKBURY, OXFORDSHIRE, OX53 9DF.
The landlords reserve the right to ask you to sod off out of their pub at any time.

"Rude, strange, and unsurprisingly empty" - *The Oxford Evening Badger*

THE MAY'S SPEECH
Christmas 2011

Hullo. I'm speaking to you from my house, because that's where I live. I hope you're having a nice Christmas. At this time of year we may reflect on faith since, of course, Christmas is firmly rooted in the Christian tradition. But someone doesn't have to believe in that faith, per se, in order to enjoy some of the more secular aspects of the Christmas period in much the same way that, for example, I can use electricity even though, in some senses, I don't truly believe in it. Actually, it rather troubles me that even the people behind electricity, inasmuch as anyone can be behind such a thing, show strange lapses in what we might term their faith. I'm referring of course to the Institution of Electrical Engineers (or IEE) standards for domestic and commercial wiring which have changed over the years, notably in 2004 when new colour codings were introduced, aimed at standardising wiring colours across much of the world but, in doing so, dictating that the live wire was now coloured brown rather than red and, personally, I find that rather confusing. The move towards green and yellow for earth made some sense (although actually, if you think about it, surely earth should be, if anything, brown?), but getting rid of red, a colour that we instinctively associate with danger, for the live seemed strange to me, notwithstanding that it reportedly caused problems for colour-blind people.

Sorry, where was I? Oh yes, Christmas. At this time of year it is, I think, important to reflect for a brief moment on the happy or joyful moments that the preceding year has brought to us. Personally, for example, I experienced great joy in early summer when I had my aeroplane serviced and the propeller cleaned. Of course, cleaning an aeroplane propeller is a bit more complicated than washing a car or even a motorcycle. Some propellers, although not the one on my aeroplane as it happens, have a special texture created by processes such as shot peening or a carefully applied anti-corrosion lacquer and these can be damaged by abrasive cloths or brushes. Likewise, simply pressure washing a propeller is inadvisable because the application of a powerful jet of water can allow moisture to penetrate the seals at the base of the propeller and this will inevitably lead to long-term problems with the mechanism that adjusts the angle of attack, which is, of course, a vital part of any aeroplane with a constant speed propeller. With this in mind, it is sensible to leave the cleaning of the propeller to experts who will use the appropriate cloths and non-alkaline cleaning solutions. Assuming that your propeller is correctly adjusted, keeping it clean will allow it to remain ideally balanced and that of course has benefits for efficiency.

Sorry, I seem to have drifted off the subject slightly. Ah yes, Christmas.

A time of year to cement the strong bond between individual members of a family in much the same way as I bonded the slowly separating sole back into place on a pair of casual shoes just yesterday. The interesting thing about modern adhesives is that they work using acrylic resins which are activated almost instantly when brought into contact with the ions in water. You might think this rather odd since the instructions on most glues specify that both surfaces are 'clean and dry', yet the truth is that the humidity in the air itself is usually enough to trigger the bonding element contained in the glue, often within seconds. Now, this is… oh, I'm being told that we're out of time.

How did that happen?

Oh well. Merry Christmas.

Winter Driving Tips

Winter roads can be particularly slippery and that can make driving more hazardous. As a result, many organisations release winter driving tips which are so searingly patronising that they make your teeth weep. Here at *Top Gear*, however, we believe that staying safe in adverse conditions isn't about keeping a flask of blankets and some tartan soup in your car; it's entirely related to what you SAY. Here, then, is the *Top Gear* guide to some phrases you should NOT use if you want to avoid an accident this festive season:

DON'T WORRY, I'VE GOT THIS ONE!

WATCH THIS!

IF IN DOUBT, HANDBRAKE!

POWEEEEEEER!

AS I ALWAYS SAY, HAMMER IT AND SEE WHAT HAPPENS!

OH IT'LL BE FINE!

RUBBISH! I CAN GET MUCH CLOSER THAN THAT!

Richard Hammond's Believe It or Not!

THE MORRIS OXFORD AND THE AUSTIN CAMBRIDGE ARE THE ONLY CARS TO TAKE PLACE IN THE ANNUAL OXFORD AND CAMBRIDGE BOAT RACE.

'YOU CAN PAINT IT ANY COLOUR YOU LIKE, SO LONG AS IT'S BLACK,' SAID CAR MANUFACTURER HENRY FORD BUT HE WASN'T TALKING ABOUT CARS - HE WAS WAS MISQUOTING THE LYRICS OF HIS FAVOURITE ROLLING STONES SONG, 'PAINT IT BLACK'.

AS WELL AS BEING AN ACTOR, MUSICIAN, AND HUMANITARIAN, STING ALSO DESIGNS CARS IN HIS SPARE TIME. HIS LATEST INVENTION, THE TOYOTA STING, IS THE ONLY CAR IN THE WORLD POWERED BY JAZZ.

THE STIG'S CHRISTMAS SPEECH

"

"

CHRISTMAS HIGHLIGHTS

Christmas Eve

Room 101
4am Dave

Joining regular host Paul Merton in this repeat of the popular show about things people hate is James May, whose pet hates include noisy idler gears, recalcitrant bearing casings and poorly sited alternators.

Come Drive With Me
5.30pm Channel 4, Channel 4 HD

A special celebrity edition where fusty James, brash Jeremy, likeable Richard and taciturn Stig all compete to make the tastiest meal IN A CAR. With hilarious and highly incendiary consequences, possibly.

The Very Best of Star in a Reasonably Priced Car
8pm BBC2

A massive compilation of clips from that bit of Top Gear you usually use as excuse to go and put the kettle on. Also features some previously unseen interviews including Amanda Holden swearing like a Viking, Moira Stuart getting into a fist fight with an audience member and the singer from Mumford & Sons careering off the track and sliding horrendously through a primary school!

Cars Britannia
11.20pm BBC4

Jeremy Clarkson takes us through the history of the British car - actually, that's a good idea for a show. Shh!

40 Years Of The Old Grey Clarkson Test
11.30pm BBC2

A tribute to this much-loved 1970s classic and the show he presented, as once more 'Shouting' Jeremy Clarkson presents four solid hours of the music he loves - in other words, one and a half tracks from a Yes album.

Christmas Day

Top Gear Christmas Day Special
7pm BBC1, BBC1 HD

In previous years, the team have been to America, the Middle East and South America, but this year's *Top Gear Special* promises to beat them all because for the first time, Jeremy, Richard, James and the Stig are heading out to Rhyl in Wales. 'We seem to have run out of money,' quips Jeremy. 'I've never been to Wales,' adds Richard, 'No, wait, yes I have.' 'I am incredibly excited,' says James, 'Rhyl has a fascinating and vibrant history that we all could learn from. No, wait, I was thinking of that other place. You know, starts with an M or maybe a J. Erm...'

The Darling Buds Of James May
7pm ITV4

Loveable, crusty old Pop Clarkson gets a surprise when it turns out Catherine Zeta-Jones was Richard Hammond in a frock all along. Not suitable for viewers in Wales. Or anywhere.

The Gearies
11.59pm BBC2

A dip into the archive for this classic episode of a great 1970s comedy show. Starring patriotic simpleton Jeremy Brooke-Clarkson, science-obsessed weirdo Graeme May and cute, cuddly Richard Oddie, The Gearies brightened the lives of children everywhere as they rode into town on their trandem and - in this legendary episode - dropped a Volkswagen from off the top of the Post Office Tower.

Boxing Day

Tales From The Top Gear Riverbank
11.30am ITV1, ITV1 HD
A repeat for this children's favourite, where cute furry animals Jeremy Clarkson the Rat, James May the Vole, and Richard Hamster, sit around beside a river and talk nonsense until one of them bursts into flames. Several animals and two insects were harmed in the making of this programme.

Last of the Summer Gear
4.30pm BBC2
A rare chance to see this unforgettable episode of the loveable sitcom where Clarkson, May and Hampo bumble around the place and test drive a tin bath on wheels. Co-starring the Stig as Nora Batty.

This Is Your Life
6pm 5, 5 HD
Another welcome rerun of this classic show, which in this episode featured *Top Gear*'s very own Jeremy Clarkson. And it's a great show - from the moment Jeremy swears uncontrollably for ten minutes after he's been shown the big red book, to his hilarious inability to remember who all these people are, and the big finale where he memorably shouts, 'You've mistaken me for PAXMAN, you idiots!'

Antiques Roadshow
6.30pm BBC1, BBC1 HD
James May shows us his new house.

Later... With Jools Holland Christmas Special
11pm BBC1, BBC1 HD
Joining the Arctic Monkeys, a reformed Pulp and singer Janelle Monae is Jools' special guest, James May, who will be talking about his general disdain for music created since 1936 and his love for Donko.

Soapwatch

EastEnders Christmas Special
8pm Christmas Day BBC1, BBC1 HD
There's a treat in store for the inhabitants of Albert Square when three strangers drive a tank into the Queen Vic, killing everyone and allowing the downtrodden locals a chance to start again, repopulating their lives with slightly more convincing Cockney stereotypes.

Coronation Street
7.30pm Christmas Day ITV1, ITV1 HD
Another tram crashes into the street, only this time it's made of wood and old hovercraft and is driven by Jeremy Clarkson who keeps shouting, 'Out of the way Northerners!'

Emmerdale
7pm (every day this week) ITV1, ITV1 HD
An eventful week as there's a surprise celebrity visitor when Richard Hammond arrives in Emmerdale. Then he realizes his mistake and gets out as quickly as possible, just before the Woolpack bursts into flames.

MISSED IT?
Don't worry! Simply flick through this magazine really fast to enjoy new VICTORIAN iPLAYER! This week: Sunday's *Top Gear*

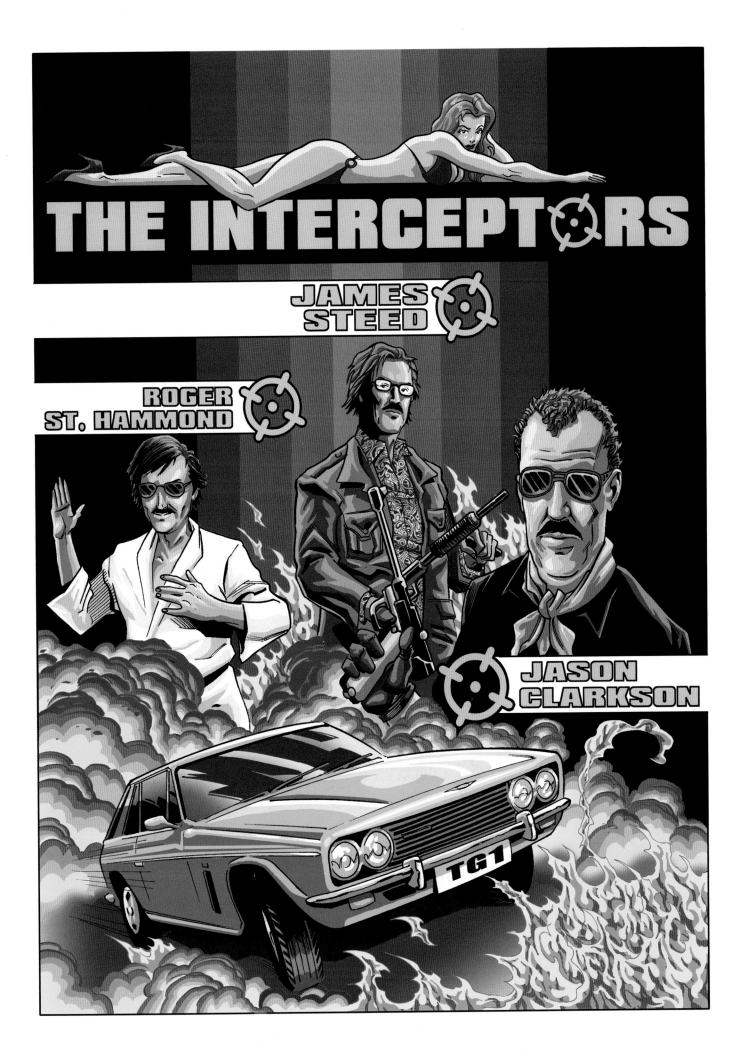

THE INTERCEPTORS

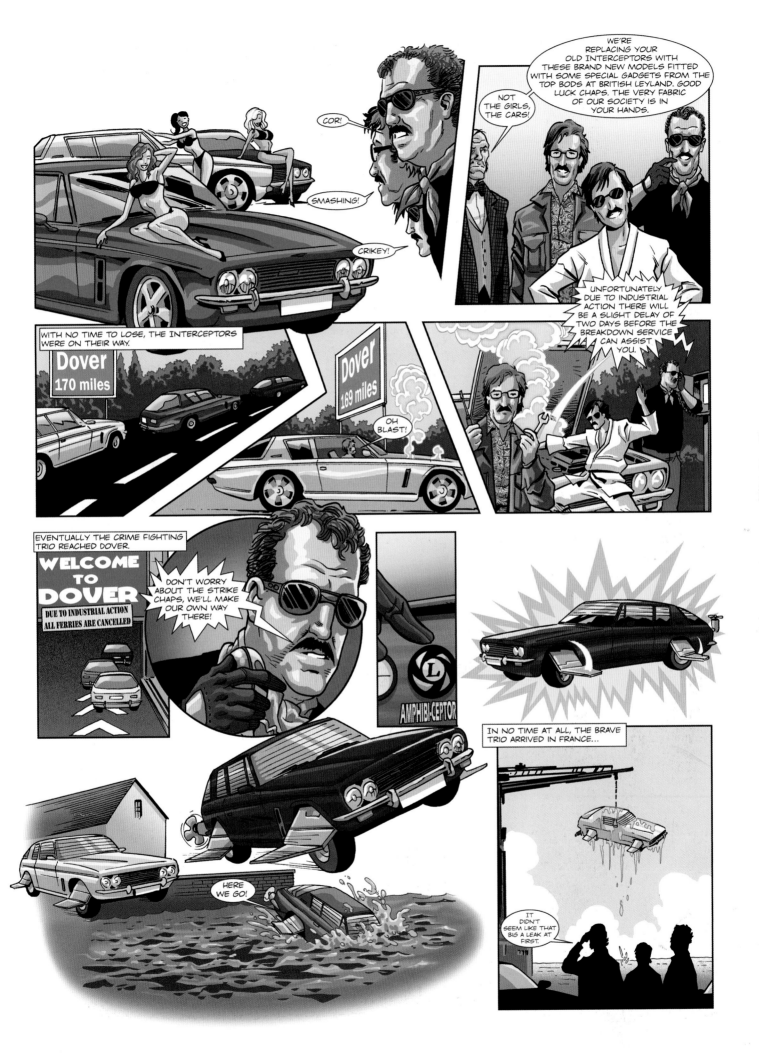

SEVEN REASONS WHY 2012
WILL BE A VERY GOOD YEAR

Here are the cars to look forward to in 2012. If they don't get delayed, that is. Which they probably will. In which case, here are the cars to look forward to in 2012, 2013 and 2014...

PAGANI HUAYRA

How do you follow an act like the certifiable Zonda? By strapping a 700bhp V12 with a whacking pair of turbos into the middle of a slippery carbon-titanium shell and giving the whole thing an entirely unpronounceable name, that's how. Capable of 0–62mph in 3.3 seconds and a top speed of 230mph, the million-euro Huayahayuara will make the Zonda look like an exercise in subtlety when it arrives in 2012.

PORSCHE 911

Who'd have thought it? Putting a four-cylinder engine in the front of the 911? Well, certainly not Porsche. Never a firm to meddle with a winning formula, the all-new 911 – codenamed 991 – sensibly sticks to the recipe of its forebears: engine in the rear, retro looks and irritatingly excellent handling. Oh, and a seven-speed manual gearbox, which is at least three more ratios than the human brain is capable of dealing with.

AUDI QUATTRO

Barking the phrase 'Fire up the Quattro!' never had quite the desired effect when the 'Quattro' in question was a four-wheel drive Audi A6 estate. But when the production version of 2011's Quattro Coupé Concept reaches the road – hopefully late in 2012 – it'll rekindle all our Ashes to Ashes fantasies. With the five-cylinder turbo from the TT-RS turned up to 400bhp and a stubby profile inspired by Gene Hunt's weekday runabout, the Quattro should become the coupé of choice for every tough-talking, unconventional Detective Chief Inspector.

ALFA 4C

The 'baby Alfa', as it shall inevitably be known, promises all the ravishing looks of the 8C Competizione with none of the ravishing price tag of the 8C Competizione. Weighing in under a tonne and powered by a fizzy little turbo petrol, the mid-engined 4C was first shown in concept form in early 2011. Will it make it onto the road before the end of 2012? Alfa bosses reckon so. Take this prediction with a pinch of salt and hope for the best.

FORD FOCUS RS

2010's Focus RS had a woefully inadequate 300bhp dribbling through its front wheels courtesy of an anaemic five-cylinder turbo. The new RS will thankfully righten its predecessor's chronic lack of speed and torque-steer by ramming a whole load more horsepowers under the bonnet. With at least 360bhp coursing vigorously through the front wheels, the MkIII RS promises to introduce a whole new generation of drivers to the joys of independently-minded steering wheels.

Erm, we don't actually know what it'll look like yet. Sorry. Probably a bit like this, but... pointier. And angrier.

JAGUAR 'E-TYPE'

Jaguar is very keen that its new compact sports car isn't referred to as the 'new E-Type', preferring that it be assessed on its own merits rather than compared to its venerable grand-daddy. Fair point. The new E-Type – a front-engined two-seater that'll be around a foot shorter than the XK – is expected to cost around £50,000 and do battle with the Porsche Cayman when it goes on sale, hopefully some time late in 2012. Hopefully.

TOYOTA FT-86

Although its release date has been slipping backwards like a rusty Citroën parked on a steep hill, we're crossing fingers, toes and other assorted dangly bits that Toyota's lightweight, rear-wheel drive coupé – which might even be badged as a Celica – will become real in 2012. A near-identical Subaru version will arrive at the same time, powered by the same four-cylinder turbo 'boxer' engine. Thrummy.

GREATER**LONDON**AUTHORITY
MAYOR'S OFFICE

January 2011

Dear Jeremy, Richard & James,

Can I start by saying that I was initially, of course, delighted to accept your munificent offer to deliver and install the *Picea abies*, the 'Norwegian spruce' if you will, to Trafalgar Square so that it might commence, as it were, its traditional Christmas duties for the customary festive month, to whit: December.

It is therefore with great sadness, nay an ennui of incalculable depth, that I must express my disappointment at the events that unfolded in our capital's most hallowed thoroughfares last month. First of all, I can see no discernable logic for the decision, however well meant, to deliver the coniferous giant upon the back of a homemade hovercraft, the sheer uncontrollability of which was manifest from the very moment it attempted forward motion, only to accelerate with great vigour in the converse direction before making contact with a telecommunications cubicle, a 'phone box' if you will, to the considerable alarm of the gentleman inside.

The erratic and vectorless procession that followed was, it seems, no less chaotic as Mr Clarkson bellowed with noisy fury regarding the need, nay the urgency, for the provision of greater power whilst Messrs Hammond and May seemed only to obfuscate the matter with a series of whimsical retorts, many involving words such as 'oaf' and 'cock', and these light-hearted but ultimately unhelpful exchanges may or may not have been instrumental in the unfortunate incident which followed, as the top of the sizeable spruce punctured the window of a shop frontage belonging to that noble provider of great sustenance to connoisseurs of the meat and pastry art. To whit: Greggs.

It seems the eventual ingress of the glorious tree and malfunctioning Cockerellian beast into Trafalgar Square was no less of a spectacle, nor any less traumatic, especially for the group of Belgian tourists whose vacationing endeavours were rudely interrupted by sudden contact with some part of the mighty spruce, an event which caused considerable mirth amongst onlookers as these stout Lowlanders performed a comical action reminiscent of the finest works of Messrs Hanna and Barbera. To whit: they fell over.

These matters are, however, mere peccadillos when seen in the broader context of the grotesque comedy that unfolded with the manifold attempts to manoeuvre the vertiginous tree from the horizontal to the vertical position. Scarcely can I bear to re-cap the multifarious calamities that befell the arboreal installation at this time except to note that the part where it caught fire was rather predictable and set-up.

I believe my disappointment has been expressed to a satisfactory degree and I leave you, gentlemen, with just one request pertaining to the damages sustained in your unsuccessful endeavours – please put Lord Nelson back together and return him to his rightful place on top of the column that bears his name. As you yourselves might say on your whimsical television programme: how hard can it be?

Yours sincerely,

Boris Johnson

Boris Johnson

FRAPTON RETAILERS' ASSOCIATION
Representing the retailers of Frapton and Lower Upperford

To Jeremy, Richard and James,

11th January 2011

Once again, thanks for supplying, installing and turning on the Christmas lights in Frapton High Street last month. Thanks also for agreeing to pay for the damage that resulted. As promised, here is an outline of what needed to be fixed or replaced after your visit:

New windows, signs, stock for Boots – £11,594
New windows, signs, stock for WH Smith – £13,677
New windows, signs, stock for Sports Direct – £35
Replacement of paving slabs damaged in explosion – £2,550
Rebuilding of public lavatories on Thorpe Street – £10,560
Repair of damage caused to clock tower by mine-clearance machine – £7,460
Clear up of damage caused by rather predictable and set-up fire – £5,650
Removal of traction engine from canal – £2,575
Clean up of horse entrails – £580
Dry-cleaning Lady Mayoress's dress – £12
Dry-cleaning Lady Mayoress's hair – £43

Thanks again!

Roger

BUCKINGHAM PALACE

Dear Jeremy, Richard and James,

The Queen has asked me to pass on her grave concerns about your recent efforts to write and produce her Christmas Message.

Her Majesty has always recorded her message from a comfortable location such as Sandringham or Buckingham Palace, and she found it wholly unnecessary to be made to undertake this year's recording in the passenger seat of a fast-moving sports car which appeared to be engaged in a race against some young men on unicycles and a small jet aeroplane. Her Majesty also disagrees with Mr Clarkson's view that the message needed to be 'made less boring' with the interspersion of some 'massive explosions'.

I'm sorry to say that The Queen also disagreed with much of Mr Clarkson's proposed content for the message, in particular the assertion that all cyclists should be drowned and the claim that Mr Hammond would be ennobled with immediate effect as 'Lord Bellend of Wales'. Furthermore, Her Majesty was baffled as to why Mr May deemed it necessary to script a lengthy segment recounting the history of the diesel-electric locomotive. She also found the fire to be rather predictable and set up.

In summary, The Queen cannot allow for her Christmas Message to be transmitted in this form. Not unless you tell her who The Stig is.

Yours sincerely,

Peter Bowlingham-Sleeves
Senior Press Secretary

He's loved by children and he has amazing powers. But how does The Stig stack up against that other legendary figure, Santa Claus?

SANTA V

Where does he live?	North Pole
How long does it take him to get around the world?	24 hours
What does he give to all children?	Presents
Who helps him?	Elves
What is his favourite food?	Mince pies
What is his favourite drink?	Sherry
What colour is his beard?	White
What is his favourite method of propulsion?	Eight reindeer
What does he do when he's not travelling quickly around the world?	Makes toys
What is his catchphrase?	Ho ho ho

S STIG

Where does he live?	**Some say... a secret cave**
How long does it take him to get around the world?	**Some say... 46 minutes**
What does he give to all children?	**Some say... meat**
Who helps him?	**Some say... a talking crow**
What is his favourite food?	**Some say... soil**
What is his favourite drink?	**Some say... weasel milk**
What colour is his beard?	**Some say... yellow & green striped**
What is his favourite method of propulsion?	**Some say... eight cylinders (or more)**
What does he do when he's not travelling quickly around the world?	**Some say... he hangs upside down in an unnerving way**
What is his catchphrase?	**Some say... erm, nothing**

Away In His Office

Away in his office, curled up in his chair,
The little James May lays down his sweet hair.
The stars in the bright sky shine on his corduroy trews,
The little James May has been at the booze.

While outside the 21st century calls,
Inside James May's head, a slow dust falls.
No internet there, no iPad or CD,
In James May's sweet dreams, it's still 1903.

While Richard and Jeremy have a go on the Wii,
James May dreams of bread pudding and nursery tea,
While they test drive new motors each and every day,
James May is all wrapped up as he rides on a sleigh.

Come Christmas Day as we play with our stuff
The Stig comes round in a massive huff
Not for him, 'Hail fellow, well met,'
All he got was a brand new helmet.

CHRISTMAS IN THE TRENCHES

In Christmas 1914, troops from opposing sides laid down their scripts and steering wheels and met in no-man's land, led by the two men depicted at the centre of this picture, Cpt. J. Clarkson from the Top Gear Regiment and Cpt. T. Needell of the 5th Gearian Unit. In this scene, Cpt. Clarkson is leading Lt. R. Hammond, Lt. J. May and Xq. Stig whilst Cpt. Needell is followed by 2nd Lt. V. Butler-Henderson and Cpt. J. Plato. The two sides met with the intention of playing a game of football before deciding that this was a boring idea and having a race instead.

*The Rollers gambolled and played
in James May's backyard.*

*Blitzen, a top-of-the-range new Roller,
just like the one Lord Alan Sugar has got.*

*James May would enthuse, absently rubbing
Donner's Silver Lady with his tweedy elbow.*

*That girl he once saw walking into Dewhurst's
made a strong impression on James May.*

In James May's backyard, the Rollers gambolled and played. There was Donner, a big old Silver Cloud. There was Blitzen, a top-of-the-range new Roller like Alan Sugar has got. And there was Cloudbase, a lovely blue open-top Roller that a popstar would have once owned before punk.

The Rollers loved their lives! Every day they'd lie in their stable until James May came down with a handful of petrol and a big old chamois leather, and he'd feed them and polish them and they'd purr silently at his affectionate, if slightly dated, touch.

"One day," James May would tell them, "One day you'll need to transport all the presents I've been making in my workshop to the orphans of the world."

And the Rollers listened, only half understanding, as James May told them of his life's mission: to bring expensive handmade toys with a nostalgic element to the parentless children of the world.

"Just think!" James May would enthuse, absently rubbing Donner's Silver Lady with his tweedy elbow, "There are little children in Soweto who've never had a game of Totopoly! Orphans in Tashkent who don't know what it's like to play with handmade alphabet bricks! And that's where you come in, my little Rollers!"

And the Rollers would listen, only slightly less intently as they'd heard this all before. In fact, it was all James May talked about, apart from the difference between the Supermarine Spitfire prototype and the actual production line model. There was that one time he'd gone a bit off topic and talked wistfully about a girl he'd once liked, who he'd seen from the top of a bus walking into Dewhurst's, but pretty soon he'd got control of his emotions and wrested the subject back to providing top-of-the-range home-made toys to orphans.

The Silver Lady, some say, is based on Richard Hammond with a sheet over his shoulders.

Rudolf, the unhappy Roller, often played alone.

"Have you got a cold?" sneered Donnor.
"You look like you're on standby" said Blitzen.

Rudolf was ashamed of his nose.
Being different was no fun at all.

But for the most part the Rollers gambolled and played in the extensive grounds of James May's ancestral home, Alton Towers. They were happy – with one exception…

Rollers, as you know, are handsome beasts. With their classic lines, their distinctive radiator grilles, and of course the Silver Lady – an image based, some say, on Richard Hammond with a sheet over his shoulders – the Roller is rightly proud of its handsome looks and glorious lineage. There was however one exception, and his name was Rudolf. In all aspects save one, Rudolf was a perfectly normal Roller, a late 1970s Camargue with soft leather interior and a pretty decent in-car stereo system.

But in the middle of the grille, which in the other Rollers was a shining chrome landscape of unblemished verticality, Rudolf – alone of all the Rollers – had a shiny red nose. A nose so shiny it gave out a light brighter than a thousand headlights. It beamed out red like a thousand "models"' windows in Soho.

The other Rollers teased Rudolf mercilessly about his red nose. "Have you got a cold?" sneered Donner. "You look like you're on standby," said Blitzen. "No," corrected Cloudbase, "He looks like a taxi that bought a red nose for Comic Relief and the driver couldn't be bothered to take it off again."

Rudolf never replied to their taunts. He knew he was just as good as them, but he was ashamed of his nose. He knew that being different was no fun at all.

"When James May gets a squad of Rollers together to deliver his handmade toys to the orphans of the world," said Donner haughtily, "do you think he'll pick you, Rudolph? With your stupid red nose like a big pimple?" Donner and the other Rollers laughed, and Rudolph went into his lonely stable and cried.

James May's Heath Robinson-inspired alarm clock woke him up on Christmas Eve morning.

James May could hardly see across the stable yard, let alone into the sky.

The Rollers gathered, many of them groggy from Blitzen's stag night, the night before.

James May saw a bright light which could illuminate any darkness.

James May's Heath Robinson-designed alarm clock fired a tiny cannon into the backside of a rubber monkey on a string, which propelled the monkey on a string across the room into a cup placed on a set of scales. The monkey's weight caused a candle on the other half of the scales to rise up and light a thin blue touchpaper, firing a small rocket at a set of dominos on a conveyor belt. The conveyor belt began to move, and as the dominos fell off its end, each one hit a tiny hammer placed against a large bell, causing it to ring. The bell rang and rang and rang until James May pulled his nightcap off his head, thrust his large feet into fluffy slippers, and got out of bed.

James May looked at his calendar. Christmas Eve! It was time! Time to initiate Operation Deliver Classy Handmade Toys To The Orphans Of The World! He dressed quickly and ran outside. But, instead of the clear crispness of a December morn like what he had been hoping before, the day lay dull and grey, wreathed in a deep glum fog. James May could hardly see across the stable yard, let alone into the sky that he had hoped to fill with darting, determined Rollers.

"Well, this is a to-do," said James May. He assembled the Rollers, many of whom were rather groggy from Blitzen's stag night the day before, and gathered them round him.

"Rollers!" he shouted, "Turn your headlights on!"

Now Rollers have excellent headlights but even the combined force of all their lights was barely enough to penetrate the gloom. Plus they all had headaches from drinking Malibu so they weren't really up for it.

"Oh no!" said James May. "My plan is doomed!"

Then he saw it. At the back of the stable, there was a light. A bright, red, burning light. A light which could illuminate any darkness.

*"Rudolf with your nose so bright,
won't you guide my sled tonight?"*

*Rudolf flew into the air, pulling the sled,
loaded with handmade gifts.*

*Rudolf, now best of friends with James May
and all the orphans in the world.*

*Next Christmas Eve, when you see a red light in
the sky, look for Rudolf and James May.*

"Of course!" shouted James May, causing several of the Rollers to groan loudly, "Rudolf!"

And he ran into the stable, to find Rudolf – bright eyed and alert, because of course nobody had invited him to Blitzen's stag – looking at him in puzzlement.

"I need you, Rudolf!" shouted James May.

"Me?" stammered Rudolf. "But n-nobody needs me. I'm a loser." James May looked down at Rudolf.

"Rudolf with your nose so bright," he said, "Won't you guide my sled tonight?' "Yes!" shouted Rudolf.

"There's no time to lose!" said James May. Together they raced outside and James May gathered all the handmade gifts he'd made for the orphans of the world and loaded them onto a sled the size of Hampshire.

"Rudolf!" he said, "Can you pull that sled?"

"Yes!" shouted Rudolf.

So James May hitched his sled to Rudolf.

"Rudolf!" he shouted, "Are you ready!"

"Yes!" shouted Rudolf.

"Will you please stop shouting?" said Donner. "I've got a head like nobody's business."

James May got behind Rudolf's steering wheel and started his engine. And Rudolf flew into the air!

That night James May and Rudolf delivered handmade gifts and toys to the orphaned children of five continents, and when they got home, James May threw all the other Rollers out. And now Rudolf is best friends with James May and all the orphans in the world.

And even now, if you look out of your window on Christmas Eve, they say you can see a red light in the sky, and if you look even more closely, you can see a Roller with a red nose, being driven by a man in a tweed jacket, pulling a sled laden with home made gifts. Because Rudolf is real, and James May is real! Either that, or you've been drinking.

THE TWELVE DAYS OF TOP GEAR CHRISTMAS

ON THE TWELFTH DAY OF CHRISTMAS MY TRUE LOVE SENT TO ME...

A TWELVE-CYLINDER FERRARI

ELEVENS ON THE ROAD

A ONE-TEN LAND ROVER

NINE LAPS OF DUNSFOLD

V8S A-REVVING

A 7-SERIES BEEMER

A SIX-SPEED GEARBOX

FIIIIIVE GOLD STIGS

FOUR COMBINES

THREE FRENCH HATCHBACKS

A TWO-CYLINDER FIAT

AND A CLARKSON IN A POWER SLIDE

Richard Hammond's

Believe It or Not!

DON'T BOTHER CHANGING YOUR MONEY INTO EUROS WHEN YOU VISIT DENMARK'S FAROE ISLANDS- BECAUSE THEY DON'T USE REGULAR MONEY AT ALL. THEIR CURRENCY IS COMPOSED ENTIRELY OF JEREMY CLARKSON'S USED OPINIONS.

THE 1996 LAMBORGHINI ESTRELLA CONCEPT CAR IS ONE OF THE MOST EXCITING EVER DESIGNED. BUILT IN THE EXACT SHAPE OF ACTRESS PENELOPE CRUZ, IT COULD ALSO GO UNDERWATER.

'JAMES MAY' IS THE NAME OF A HUGELY POPULAR GAME SHOW IN SWEDEN. ITS NAME ROUGHLY TRANSLATES AS 'JAMES MAY'

JAMES MAY

3 RANTS

1 RANT

3 APPLES 4 SNORTS

1lb TOMATOES 2 PONTIFICATES

SPECIAL OFFER 4 BLUSTERS

All I want for Christmas...

SNOW WHITE ON THE SEVEN CARS

Christmas is a time for family, festivity… and covering things in white in the spurious belief it makes them look a bit 'snowy'. Accordingly, here are our seven favourite modern cars that look best in cheery, Christmassy white…

KOENIGSEGG AGERA R

The problem with most hypercars is that they're entirely impractical for ski trips, on account of their paltry luggage space. But the Agera R is different. With its streamlined carbon fibre roofbox — perfect for storing your carbon fibre skis, carbon fibre ski boots and carbon fibre ski instructor — this is a truly practical 1,100bhp family hypercar. In fact, if it wasn't for the small matter of 550bhp coursing through each rear wheel, this could be the perfect ski trip vehicle. And what better way to blend in subtly in Courchevel, Verbier or the Milton Keynes snowdome than by painting your practical family hypercar in cheery, snowy white?

RANGE ROVER EVOQUE

Land Rover describes the Evoque — unquestionably the most desirable little SUV in the history of the universe — as 'highly customisable'. This translates as 'go on, do your worst. Feel free to entirely ruin your Evoque by ordering it with a hideous colour combination. At least it'll be unique!' Faced with the Evoque's dizzying choice of shades for the body, roof and cabin, the sensible choice is to spec what the Land Rover marketing men call the 'James May Las Vegas Special': white-on-white with a cross-dressing Cher impersonator on the back seat.

LAMBORGHINI AVENTADOR

The Aventador gets Lamborghini's first all-new V12 since the 350GT of 1963. Yes, that's right: every previous V12 Lambo, from the Miura to the Murcielago, used essentially a variation on the same venerable 'Bizzarini' engine. But just because it's got a shiny new 6.5-litre engine doesn't mean the Aventador needs some new-fangled, 21st-century colour scheme. Oh no. Best deck out your Aventador in retina-scrambling white and be entirely unapologetic about all its noise and power and speed. And what speed: the Aventador will do 217mph flat-out, and went round the *Top Gear* test track in 1:16:5, faster than a Veyron Super Sport.

VW GOLF GTI

Proudly getting lost in snowdrifts since 1981, the venerable Golf GTI is the original, and greatest, hot hatch. It may have put on a few pounds and got a little pokier over the last three decades – the MkI GTI developed only 110bhp but weighed just over 800kg, compared to the 232bhp and 1,300kg of the latest 'Edition 35' model – but the GTI still remains pretty much the most fun you can have in a front-drive car. And, if you spec it right, it's still one of the coolest. Off the top of our heads, we'd go for, ooh... candy white paint, with red-detailed wheels, houndstooth interior and a knobbly golf ball on top of the gearlever. Please.

SSC TUATARA

Too-ta-ra? Twitterer? Twa-tarra? However it's pronounced, this is the latest hypersonic hero from Shelby Super Cars – the tiny American firm that, in 2005, snatched the production car land speed record when its Ultimate Aero hit 256mph in Washington state, eclipsing the Veyron's 254mph. Of course, Bugatti bit back, with the help of James May and the 1,200bhp Veyron SS, to raise the bar to 268mph, but SSC reckons its Tuataurautara can go even faster. Exactly how fast, we don't yet know. But we do know this: it looks damn fine in pearly white. Not that we've seen it in any other colour yet, mind. It'll probably look pretty good in black. Or yellow. Or...

LEXUS LFA

It is a truth universally acknowledged that fast Japanese cars look best in white. Scientists have spent decades trying to discover why this is, but it remains a mystery of nature, like the extinction of the dinosaurs, or Dale Winton. And Japanese cars don't come much faster than the tech-laden, freakishly noisy Lexus LFA. Packing a 5.0-litre V10 that revs to an unprecedented 9,500rpm, it'll launch all the way to 200mph, causing lasting damage to your Eustachian tube as it goes. If you've got £330,000 down the back of the sofa, you should (a) buy a white LFA immediately and (b) seriously consider why you have such a large sofa and such a lax attitude to loose change.

BMW 1-SERIES M COUPE

'I haven't driven anything this perfect since the original Golf GTI!' bellowed Sir Jeremy of Clarkson when he tested the tiny, tyre-smoking 1M. With 340bhp, rear-wheel drive and unashamedly tail-focused handling, there's little to dislike about the smallest car from BMW's M-division. *Top Gear* loves the 1M so much that we would take it painted with an enamelled compound of the snot scraped from the underside of a year-9 maths class desk. But ideally we'll have it in cool, classy white to show off its Bulging Arches and Muscular Haunches (©Autocar, ad infinitum) to best effect.

IF *TOP GEAR* MADE SANTA'S SLEIGH...

Missiles as a counter measure against present thieves

Bugatti Veyron engine to achieve speed for take off, connected to chunky Land Rover wheels

Barbecue. Well, there's no need for reindeer to pull this sleigh but they do make delicious burgers

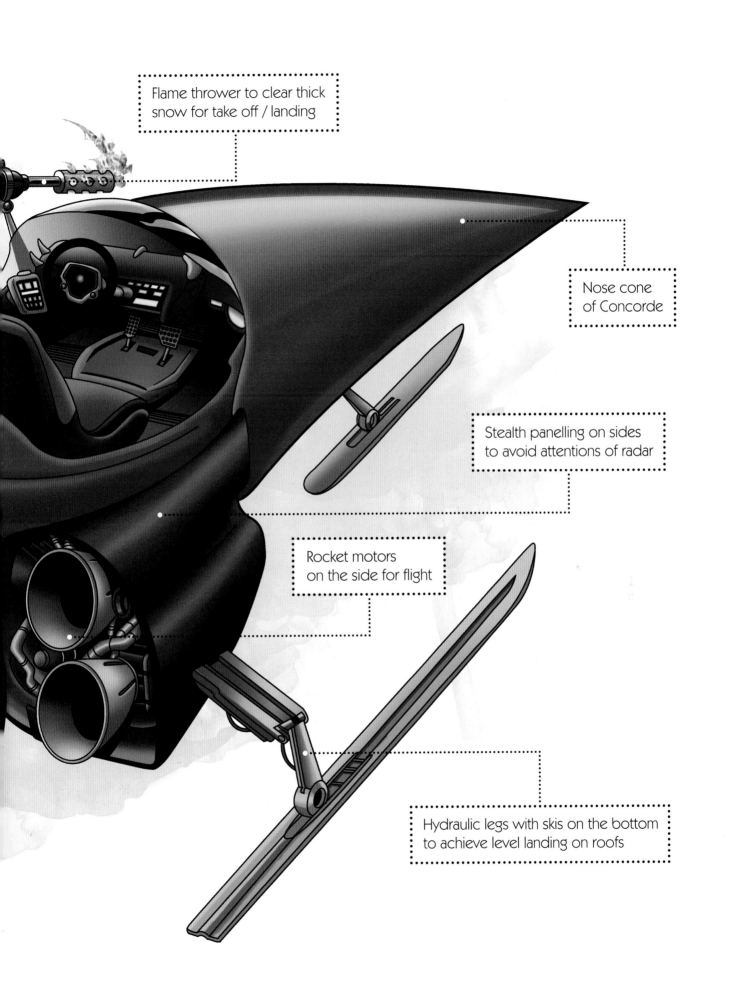

Flame thrower to clear thick
snow for take off / landing

Nose cone
of Concorde

Stealth panelling on sides
to avoid attentions of radar

Rocket motors
on the side for flight

Hydraulic legs with skis on the bottom
to achieve level landing on roofs

TOP GEAR ALMANAC · 2012 ·

JANUARY

It will be very cold. But not as cold as February. You mark my words! The most important recycling event of the year will take place, as thousands of men go to Marks & Spencer and swap awful clothes that didn't even fit them, for slightly different, marginally less awful clothes that do.

Richard Hammond will buy a new motorcycle with tokens from his aunt.

FEBRUARY

Cold, isn't it? Told you! February is the month of Valentine's Day, when young lovers will give each other gifts of chocolate, champagne and roses, and older lovers will give each other jumpers from Marks & Spencer that still don't fit.

MARCH

Large areas of South East Asia will be devastated by floods. War will break out somewhere in the Middle East. And somebody will die in *EastEnders*, only to be replaced by someone who had a top ten hit in 1984.

Jeremy Clarkson will awaken from his six-week festive stupor to write a column about how they should put gin in milk, like they did in the old days.

APRIL

'April is the cruelest month,' someone once said. But who cares? It's a month. I mean, it's not like it's going to have its days taken into care, is it? Anyway, on the calendar you got from an elderly relative, April will be a kitten in a fruit bowl. April also marks the birthdays of St George and Hitler. An expensive month for *Daily Mail* readers.

MAY

Beware Greeks bearing gifts. It might be George Michael and his latest album. If you don't like it, the only way you can get him to take it back is to construct a massive wooden horse, put the CD inside it and then leave the horse on Hampstead Heath. NEAR HIS HOUSE.

JUNE

Summer solstice. A time when hundreds of models from West London will stand around wearing floral wellies and looking a bit lost because there's no Glastonbury Festival this year. The reason the event is not being held in 2012 is because Coldplay were due to headline but no one could get hold of the Pagan god of vaguely swaying whilst holding a lighter in the air.

The Stig will contemplate revealing his true identity, but June is a bad month for landing lucrative publishing contracts.

JULY

Following an astonishing victory at Wimbledon, Andy Murray will wake up and cry a bit. In other news, July is when summer really kicks in. 'PHEW! WHAT A SCORCHER!' screams the *Daily Telegraph* front page alongside a photo of a smashing young filly in her beachwear. Meanwhile the *Star* will print a photograph of a young couple at it like knives on the beach. Sales of pre-knotted handkerchiefs will go through the roof.

AUGUST

The Notting Hill Carnival will take place in West London. On the first day, a fat black lady and a tall white policeman will dance together as they do every year, while the lady says, 'Leave her, Kevin, you don't love her,' and the policeman replies, 'You know I can't, Alison, it would break her heart.' Later they will have guilty, furtive sex back at the police station. Probably.

SEPTEMBER

Kids will go back to school and television executives will return from their holidays in Tuscany, hopped up on Chianti and awful ideas for reality TV shows. One of the shows – HELP! MY HAIRY FACED BROTHER IS A SKY TV COMMISSIONING EXECUTIVE – will be a surprise flop.

James May will get the blankets and the thick duvet down from the attic.

OCTOBER

Is it Autumn yet? It must be, as no leaves will have fallen from the trees and it will still be rather warm. Some flying ants will get their wires crossed, and have to fly around Somerset pretending they were visiting relatives in the West Country.

Jeremy Clarkson will finish his latest book, but forget to take it back to the library on time, landing him with a fine of 23p.

NOVEMBER

Guy Fawkes will be burned in bonfires all across the nation. As the flames envelop him, he'll scream, 'I would have gotten away with it if it hadn't been for you darn kids!' A tidal wave will sweep Peru into the sea. A sort of dragon thing will attack Tokyo, destroying thousands of model helicopters. *Coronation Street* will court controversy when a straight family takes over the Rovers.

DECEMBER

Everyone in Britain will calmly and cheerfully set out to post the Christmas cards they've already written in the envelopes they addressed weeks ago. Then they will wrap and post the presents they sensibly bought during the summer. Nobody at all will panic and run around the house screaming, 'OH MY GIDDY CRAP! I HAVEN'T BOUGHT ANY PRESENTS AND IT'S CHRISTMAS EVE!!!' No, that will not happen. No siree. The Queen's Speech will come from a solid-gold space rocket orbiting the earth, before departing for the Royal Family's home planet of Saxe-Coburg 6.

The Stig will find God and enter a silent order of monks. James May will enjoy success as his recession-proof board game Donko! is a surprise hit. Richard Hammond will settle down to watch all the Christmas telly he's recorded, only to find he's pressed the wrong button and got 56 hours of *Two Pints Of Lager* instead. Jeremy Clarkson will receive a letter asking him if he'd consider becoming Britain's next official National Treasure when Stephen Fry retires.

FASTEST

things around the world*

If, in a theoretical universe, various things could get around the world in one go without stopping, which would be fastest?

SANTA'S SLEIGH

Top speed: 100,000mph

Time around the world: 14 minutes, 24 seconds

Santa doesn't release official figures on sleigh performance, but given the number of stops he has to make we estimate that it's pretty nippy.

SPACE SHUTTLE

Top speed: 17,500mph

Time around the world: 1 hour, 30 minutes

These are Official NASA figures for a Shuttle in orbit.

LOCKHEED SR-71 BLACKBIRD

Top speed: 2,193mph

Time around the world: 11 hours, 21 minutes

This is the official speed record set by an SR-71. It could probably go faster but if they'd told you they'd have to kill you.

CONCORDE

Top speed: 1,350mph

Time around the world: 18 hours, 27 minutes

Concordes did go faster than this, but the figure quoted was the regular max cruising speed.

AIRBUS A380

Top speed: 560mph

Time around the world: 1 day, 20 hours, 27 minutes

All of the machines here would need refuelling on their journey but the A380, at 9,548 miles between pit stops, has the greatest range.

BUGATTI VEYRON SUPERSPORT

Top speed: 268mph

Time around the world: 3 days, 20 hours, 54 minutes

Obviously this depends on there being massive bridges across major oceans. We've checked and sadly there aren't.

WALKING

Top speed: 3½ mph

Time around the world: 42 weeks, 2 days, 10 hours, 42 minutes

This is very theoretical because of course in real life you'd have to stop a few times to have a sleep and preferably a shower.

JAMES MAY'S CARAVAN AIRSHIP

Top speed: 2mph

Time around the world: Infinite

Speed is irrelevant here because it never goes in the direction that James, or indeed anyone else, intends it to.

Distance around the world:
24,901½ miles

* In theory

TOP GEAR TIMELINE

CHRISTMAS IS A TIME FOR LOOKING BACK AT THE PAST – SO WHAT BETTER OPPORTUNITY COULD THERE TO REEL IN THE YEARS AND TUG ON THE FRANKLY EPIC TIMELINE OF CLASSIC MOMENTS IN TOP GEAR HISTORY?

1492

Christopher Columbus discovers America, even though everyone had managed perfectly well without it for several years. Once again the world changes, as *Top Gear* presenters now have the chance to go on epic, pointless road trips across the USA, with lots of close-ups of shimmering highways and cow skulls lying in the desert that no way did a props master just put there.

2011 BC

The invention of the wheel is dismissed by new presenter James May as a fad.

1002 BC

The new horses are tested, with the stocky but reliable Przwalski's Horse coming in for particular praise, even though its one-horse-power engine isn't that fast.
Early presenter Ug the Cave Man is suspended for making favourable comments about this year's Pirelli Cave Painting Calendar.

1066

A change of style as not only is the show revamped, losing some no-longer-popular regular items, but also William of Normandy invades England, changing our language and culture for ever. French words, manners and customs become prevalent, as do those little cars that geography teachers drive.

44 BC

Swooning amongst the ladies in the audience as this week's Star in a Reasonably Priced Chariot is Cliff Richard. And controversy as the first Stig throws off his white helmet and reveals himself to be popular chariot racer Ben Hur. Presenter James May looks at the new Roman roads and declares them to be a fad.

1588

Spain attempts to flood the UK with cheap, underpriced galleons but the plan fails when they all sink coming off the ferry near Plymouth. James May sees the whole thing while playing a game of bowls, which he declares slightly too exciting. The bowls, that is, not the Spanish Armada.

1843

Top Gear covers the Great Exhibition at the Crystal Palace, where visitors gasp at examples of craftsmanship and skill from the different corners of the Empire, each one of which has a dolly bird in a bikini lying on it.

1743

All England is enthralled as coffee houses become the in thing. A small child called Murray Walker falls into a vat of coffee and for the rest of his life is only able to communicate in short bursts of excited shouting and bouts of weird buzzing noises.

1837

Top Gear has its first royal guest, the new Queen, Victoria. Speaking English with a thick German accent, she vows that her truest aim and duty to her subjects will be Vorsprung durch Technik.

Vorsprung durch Technik

1803

Great excitement as the Star in a Reasonably Priced Warship is revealed to be navy idol Lord Nelson. Girls scream and crash-barriers collapse as Nelson, possibly confused after too much grog, becomes over-excited and declares, 'Kiss me, Hammond'.

1814

The steam train is unveiled on a Top Gear Special. James May declares it a fad, saying that passengers will die if the train goes faster than 30mph. Later he admits that he had just watched the movie Speed and got confused.

1856

Thanks to massive public subscription, Lord Nelson finally gets his own column. Jeremy Clarkson is said to be jealous.

1943

The fortunes of the Allies turn about when the Russians defeat the Germans at the battle of Stalingrad, laying the foundations for the Soviet dominance of Eastern Europe and the hated dictatorship of the Lada. Meanwhile, in England, rationing means that Jeremy Clarkson is restricted to only four outrageous remarks a month.

1861

The internal combustion engine is invented. James May, not asked for his opinion, goes into a sulk.

1933

Germany elects a new Chancellor who promises an age of ruthless efficiency, humorless dominance of the world, and really good cars that can go very fast on purpose-built motorways. Top Gear watches as the first VW Beetle is unveiled by its creator, Doktor Ferdinand My Other Car's a Porsche.

1914

Trouble on set when the first European Star in a Reasonably Priced Car – the Archduke Ferdinand – is assassinated as he comes round Gambon Corner. The ensuing political crisis soon escalates into all-out war, enabling Richard Hammond to join a bantam battalion.

1926

New presenter Noel Coward is suspended by the fledgling British Broadcasting Company for calling Norfolk very flat.

1956

France conducts secret hydrogen bomb tests in the pacific. The explosion can be heard hundreds of miles away. A similar thing happens in Britain when James May hears 'Rock Around the Clock' for the first time.

2011

The event of the year unites the nation as, in front of the great and the good at St Paul's Cathedral, a new Stig is announced.

1969

The first man lands on the Moon. His resemblance to The Stig is not noticed until many years later. Meanwhile, as Swinging London becomes a memory, the last Mini with a Union Jack on the roof is sold to an American collector, to be broken down and made into an Austin Powers movie.

2001

Distressed that the film 2001: A Space Odyssey has utterly failed to come true, Richard Hammond puts himself into suspended animation until its sequel, 2010, comes true.

1979

Sadness in the Clarkson household as Jeremy's favourite decade comes to an end.

1997

Things can only get better, promises the first New Labour Prime Minister, Tony Blair. And yet the Ford Ka continues in production.

1983

The Falkland Islands are invaded by Argentina, disturbing James May's annual holiday.

1989

The Berlin Wall comes down, revealing the sheer horror of the Trabant.

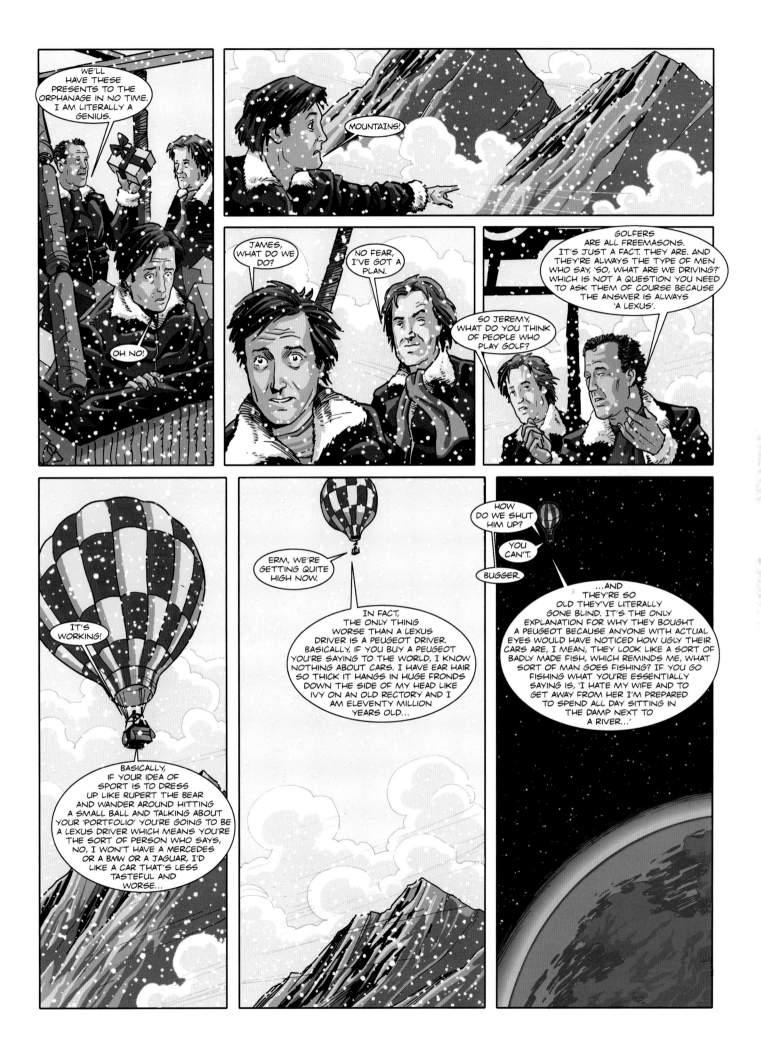

New on DVD this Christmas...

Yes, this brand new DVD from *Top Gear*'s very own professor of unintelligence is GUARANTEED to reduce your IQ within two hours!

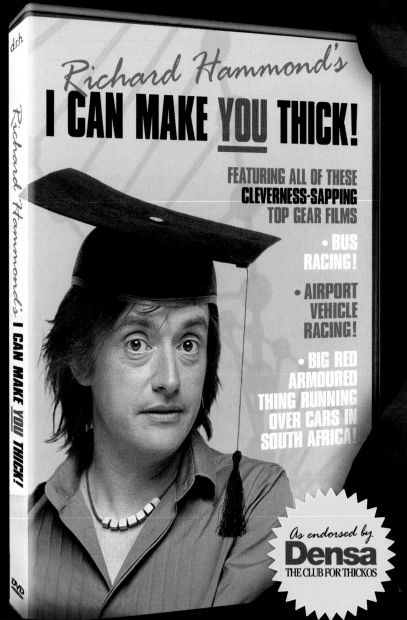

Richard Hammond's
I CAN MAKE YOU THICK!

FEATURING ALL OF THESE CLEVERNESS-SAPPING TOP GEAR FILMS

- BUS RACING!
- AIRPORT VEHICLE RACING!
- BIG RED ARMOURED THING RUNNING OVER CARS IN SOUTH AFRICA!

As endorsed by
Densa
THE CLUB FOR THICKOS

About Dr Richard Hammond:

He is NOT a real doctor!

He is from the home of unintelligence, BIRMINGHAM!

He has perfected a system for making YOU less intelligent using a complex blend of unchallenging set-ups, nonsensical story arcs, and mindless vehicular destruction, all adding up to a POTENT formula that will allow you to FEEL your brain cells LEAVING your head!

Don't just take our word for it!
Have a look at these testimonies from once-intelligent people who have benefited from the Dr Richard Hammond IQ reduction system!

'I used to know how the entire universe was made. Then I watched Richard Hammond's IQ-reducing DVD. Now I can barely understand how doors work.'

Professor Stephen Hawking

'I was getting bored making programmes about opera and literature so I watched Richard Hammond's right good DVD and now I just spend all day throwing rocks at a tree.'

Melvyn Bragg

'The very building blocks of human life fascinated me. That is until I watched Richard Hammond's brain-shrivelling DVD. Now I can waste hours at a time just staring at cows. They're dead funny.'

Lord Winston

JAMES MAY'S
CHRISTMAS GIFTS FOR CHILDREN

There's no need to buy your children an X-Pod 365 computer games system or a fancy BMX-style bicycle this Christmas. Just take a hint from Uncle James and get them one of these smashing presents.

A TANGERINE

Full of fruity goodness and with enough segments for the whole family to have a piece, the tangerine is a taste of the exotic. Better yet, it's good for you! Plus, once your children have unwrapped it, they get to unwrap it all over again thanks to nature's own waxy, orange wrapping paper! This really is the gift that keeps on giving. Although don't buy one too far in advance of Christmas or it might start to smell and look a bit funny.

A LUMP OF COAL

A practical, versatile classic that any child will enjoy! A lump of coal can be anything your son or daughter's imagination want it to be, from a paperweight to a shapeless space ship, from a new pet to an instrument with which to bludgeon their stupid Victorian parents to death. And of course, when the excitement gets too much, it can be burnt for warmth. Really, is there anything a lump of coal can't do? Although do please remember to wash your hands after handling.

A PICTURE OF A DOG

Your children may have requested a real dog, but real dogs can be terribly messy. Also, they make a noise and put a not-inconsiderable strain on the household food budget. Plus, youngsters frequently lose interest in an oft-requested item once they are in possession of it, which will leave you with the bothersome task of having to dispose of it in a way that will not attract the attentions of the authorities. Happily, with a picture of a dog your children will get all the joy of looking at an actual dog for as long as they find this interesting, after which you can simply pop the picture of the dog into a cupboard, safe in the knowledge that this will not lead your neighbours to complain about all the muffled barking.

A SPINNING TOP

Your children will be amazed and delighted the first time they realise that the brightly coloured cone they have just unwrapped isn't the pocket-sized electronic music player they had asked for and is in fact something much more exciting. It is a thing that spins round at an initially high rate of revolutions per minute which then slowly diminishes until such a point as the device achieves a wobbly imbalance and then falls over. Wow! Don't use it too much. You'll wear it out.

AN AMUSING HAT

There isn't a child alive that wouldn't want to receive a small, woollen hat as a present but this small, woollen hat is special because it has an amusing story attached to it. It's just here, pinned to the inside of the hem... oh dear, the story appears to have fallen off leaving just a rather forlorn looking safety pin. Hmph. Everyone just stay still for a moment, the story could be somewhere on the floor... No. No, I'm afraid it's gone. Well that's a shame. Rather a good story it was too. I seem to remember it involved a cat that could do maths. Oh well.

DONKO

The greatest game ever invented, from the halcyon days of the Empire. Handcrafted in the best of British oak, so portable that it can be played on a steamer trunk, Donko is the game of Kings. Can you craven you mayster before the osslebridge is collahed? Who knows. The rules were lost some time in the late 19th century! This charming game is certain to enjoy a resurgence just as soon as James gets BBC commissioners to accept his proposal for *Celebrity Donko*!

SNOW WHITE
ON THE SEVEN OLD CARS

Dreaming of a white Christmas, but couldn't give a damn whether it snows or not? Feast your eyes on our bakers' dozen of classic cars that look best in festive, snowy white…

JAGUAR E-TYPE

Any description of the drop-dead gorgeous E-Type must, by law, include Enzo Ferrari's glowing endorsement of the giant-bonneted Jag. 'The E-Type is the most beautiful car ever made,' swooned the notoriously unswooning Enzo when the Jag was launched in 1961. What most historians forget to point out is that Enzo went on to say, '…so long as eez painted in white. White, eez lovely. To be-ah honest with you, it looks-a bloody stupid in blue. Or black. Or red. What crazy bugger would buy this car in red? Get me an espresso. Pronto.'*

*May not be strictly historically accurate

BMW 3.0 CSL BATMOBILE

With its GCSE Metalwork aero kit, the CSL might have the faint whiff of an ambitious aftermarket conversion, but it's actually a deadly serious, bona fide BMW. A homologation special to allow the ever-competitive Bavarians to compete in touring car racing, the 200bhp CSL was lightweight and lethal. Only 500 CSLs made it the UK, all constructed of ultra-thin steel and aluminium, with anything that might be construed as 'unnecessary' or 'comfortable' unceremoniously removed. You think you know what we're going to say next, don't you? You think we're going to say 'And it looks best in white'. Well, we're not. We're going to say, 'And it looks best in white… with discreet Martini stripes'. So there.

TOYOTA 2000GT

Widely regarded as the first-ever Japanese supercar, the curvetastic 2000GT was introduced in 1967 to widespread acclaim and the sound of a million copies of *Easy Jokes About Japanese Cars* being ripped up. With a 145bhp straight-six, the 2000GT was capable of a deranged 135mph, which, if you take inflation into account, translates as over a million miles an hour in today's money. Only 337 were ever built, making the odds of picking up a bargain 2000GT in your local paper somewhat long. As James Bond, who drove a convertible version in *You Only Live Twice*, will himself attest, the 2000GT only really makes sense in one colour, and that's – you've guessed where we're going with this one, haven't you?

FORD ESCORT RS TURBO

Top Gear would hate to be accused of generalising (we'll leave that to the French), but the Eighties classic that is the Escort RS Turbo does have a – how to put this? – definite geographical attachment to a certain English country. Specifically, the one above Kent and below Sussex, just to the right of London. Yes, Essex. Since 1984, the all-white, squared-off, 124bhp Escort RS Turbo has been as much a feature of that upstanding county as over-white stilettos, over-white teeth and, er, a impressive record of producing excellent Test opening batsmen. Apart from its sheer, radiant coolness, the other advantage of having your RS Turbo in white is that you can cheaply fill in the inevitable rust-holes with Tippex.

FERRARI 250 SWB

In 2009, popular flame-barneted disc jockey Chris Evans paid £5.5 million for a 1961 Ferrari 250, one of just 55 ever built in convertible guise. Evans's V12 Ferrari – which in its prime developed 280bhp – was perfect in every regard but one: it was painted the wrong colour. His 250 was decked out in black, a fatal flaw we wish someone had pointed out to him before he spent all that money. Of course, what the ginger media mogul really wanted was a 250 SWB in glorious, glossy white, a paint scheme that instantly marks out its deep-pocketed driver as the very finest sort of deep-pocketed bounder.

LAMBORGHINI COUNTACH

To be honest, even if your Countach was camoflauged under a photo-realistic fresco of the street-scene directly behind it, this wedgy monster would still attract attention like Hulk Hoganwandering into a Women's Institute bridge night. Marcello Gandini's pointy, cab-forward creation is still the most outrageous bit of supercar design ever executed, and it should be considered an act of treason to own one in any colour that might be described as 'understated' or 'socially acceptable'. We shall take ours in Miami pimp-spec white, please, with the giant rear wing.

HONDA NSX TYPE-R

The mid-engined NSX Type R was developed by the Official Greatest F1 Driver of All Time, Ayrton Senna. This means that (a) it handles like a heavily greased ferret and (b) if it is ever overtaken, it will attempt to ram the offending car into a lump of Armco. The Type R version of the mid-engined NSX was 120kg lighter than the standard NSX, thanks to a neurotic weight-saving strategy from the Honda engineers, who chucked out the spare tyre, audio system and even the traction control system, and replaced the leather boot around the base of the gearshifter with a piece of lightweight mesh. Regarding colour choice, please refer to every other good, fast, Japanese car in history.

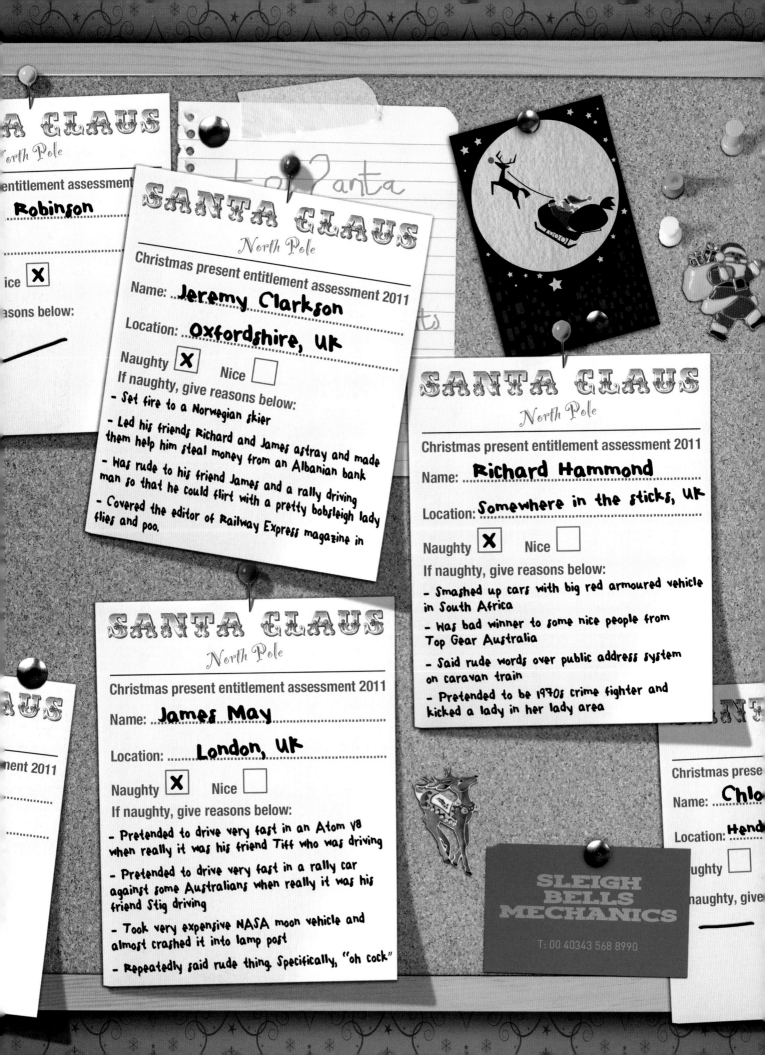

SANTA CLAUS
North Pole

Christmas present entitlement assessment 2011

Name: **Jeremy Clarkson**

Location: **Oxfordshire, UK**

Naughty **[X]**   Nice **[ ]**

If naughty, give reasons below:

- Set fire to a Norwegian skier

- Led his friends Richard and James astray and made them help him steal money from an Albanian bank

- Was rude to his friend James and a rally driving man so that he could flirt with a pretty bobsleigh lady

- Covered the editor of Railway Express magazine in flies and poo.

SANTA CLAUS
North Pole

Christmas present entitlement assessment 2011

Name: **Richard Hammond**

Location: **Somewhere in the sticks, UK**

Naughty **[X]**   Nice **[ ]**

If naughty, give reasons below:

- Smashed up cars with big red armoured vehicle in South Africa

- Was bad winner to some nice people from Top Gear Australia

- Said rude words over public address system on caravan train

- Pretended to be 1970s crime fighter and kicked a lady in her lady area

---

SANTA CLAUS
North Pole

Christmas present entitlement assessment 2011

Name: **James May**

Location: **London, UK**

Naughty **[X]**   Nice **[ ]**

If naughty, give reasons below:

- Pretended to drive very fast in an Atom V8 when really it was his friend Tiff who was driving

- Pretended to drive very fast in a rally car against some Australians when really it was his friend Stig driving

- Took very expensive NASA moon vehicle and almost crashed it into lamp post

- Repeatedly said rude thing. Specifically, "oh cock"

A CLAUS
North Pole

entitlement assessment

Robinson

ice **[X]**

asons below:

Christmas present

Name: **Chlo**

Location: **Hend**

ughty **[ ]**

naughty, give

SLEIGH BELLS MECHANICS

T: 00 40343 568 8990

---

ment 2011

TopGear

A Pantomime

CURTAIN RAISES

Young DICK HAMMONDINGTON, accompanied by his faithful dog Teegee, is walking along in the countryside.

DICK HAMMONDINGTON: Ah, what a glorious day. The sun is shining and I'm on my way to London to seek my fortune in television presenting. But wait! What's this? It looks like a sort of lamp! I wonder what will happen if I rub it?

He rubs the lamp. There is a flash and a puff of smoke.

THE JEREMY appears.

THE JEREMY: I am The Jeremy of the Lamp and I can grant you literally one million wishes.

DICK: One million?

JEREMY: Alright, three.

DH: Pffft. You can't grant me wishes.

JEREMY: Yes I can, after all…

AUDIENCE: How hard can it be!?

DICK: Alright then, I'd like an amphibious car.

JEREMY: Very well. Wait here a second…

THE JEREMY disappears off stage. There is the sound of sawing, hammering and breaking glass.

JEREMY: *(off stage)* Oh for God's sake. Hang on. Right… yes. Oh no! Flames! Those are flames! No, hang on, I've got it now. Here we go.

THE JEREMY comes back onto the stage pushing a small pick-up truck that has been crudely converted into an amphibious car. His genie hat is smouldering.

JEREMY: Yeeees! Look at that! Bask in the balmy waters of my excellence.

DICK: What's that?

JEREMY: An amphibious car.

DICK: It's rubbish. And that fire was extremely predictable and contrived.

JEREMY: Shut up.

DICK: Alright, let's see what kind of mess you can make of my second wish. I'd like someone who can get me to London really fast.

JEREMY: Wait, have you had your teeth whitened?

DICK: Get on with it.

JEREMY: Someone to get you to London really fast? That's easy.

*THE JEREMY turns to look at the audience from a slightly
different angle.*

JEREMY: Some say that in his world 'Christmas' means a type of
           photocopier. And that he loves to receive Christmas cards
           because he likes the taste. All we know is, altogether now…

AUDIENCE: He's called The Stig!

There is another flash and a puff of smoke.

THE STIG appears.

DICK: Who's he?

JEREMY: This man… well, we think he's a man… this man will get you to
           London faster than anyone in the world.

DICK: How?

JEREMY: In a supercar.

DICK: I don't have a supercar.

JEREMY: Well you didn't ask for one.

DICK: Well how was I supposed… oh never mind. It's a beautiful day,
           I'll just walk.

JEREMY: You know you've got one wish left?

DICK: I'm not interested.

JEREMY: Are you sure? I can make anything happen.

DICK: Anything? Hmm. Okay then…

DICK HAMMONDINGTON whispers in THE JEREMY's ear.

JEREMY: Really? That's what you want?

DICK: Yes.

JEREMY: Very well.

There is another flash and a puff of smoke.

JAMES MAY appears.

JAMES MAY: Hullo.

DICK: Oh for God's sake. When I said I wanted a massive

All I want for Christmas...

We Three Kings

We three kings of *Top Gear* are,
Devoting our lives to the motor car,
Even if be it,
Some kind of Fiat,
We're not particular.

We three kings of *Top Gear* are,
We'll talk about Audi or Jaguar,
Ford Granada,
Mini or Lada,
Any car, any car.

We three kings of *Top Gear* are,
We're quite prepared to go too far,
Loud or gently,
Rolls or Bentley,
We'll go for the jugular.

What is a turkey?

The turkey is as much a symbol of Christmas as Santa Claus, mistletoe and pretending to like your relatives. But what is this mysterious beast? Thankfully, *Top Gear*'s own countryside correspondent Richard Hammond is on hand to reveal the amazing secrets behind this delicious creature.

Top 10 turkey facts:

• The most common name for turkeys is Steven!

• The turkey's natural predators are wasps, otters and Beyoncé!

• The world's most famous turkey is Steven Leonburger who was United States Secretary of Defence from 1989 right up until 1992 when he was shot and eaten!

• There are no turkeys in Turkey! As a result, the word 'turkey' in Turkish means 'highly ironic'!

• The most famous turkey in Britain is Steven Williams. He was mayor of Chichester for nine years before being shot and eaten!

• The turkey is a type of fish!

• The turkey can run at up to 480mph, but only up stairs!

• The turkey can 'see' smells!

• In Portugal the turkey is considered hilarious! In a recent survey over 60% of all stand-up comedians in Lisbon were turkeys!

• The Norse word for turkey is 'janetjackson'. Bad news for the American singer of the same name who struggles to sell any records in Scandinavia as a result.

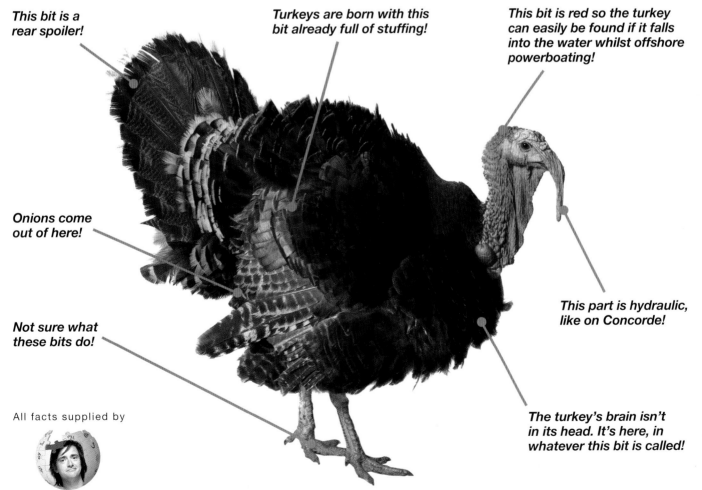

This bit is a rear spoiler!

Turkeys are born with this bit already full of stuffing!

This bit is red so the turkey can easily be found if it falls into the water whilst offshore powerboating!

Onions come out of here!

Not sure what these bits do!

This part is hydraulic, like on Concorde!

The turkey's brain isn't in its head. It's here, in whatever this bit is called!

All facts supplied by

RICHARDPEDIA
The information website for Richards!

Richard Hammond's GUIDE TO CHRISTMAS JUMPERS

THE RETINA DAMAGER

Violently clashing colours arranged in a brain scrambling formation of triangles? What you've got there is a classic Retina Damager jumper. Final proof that Auntie Jane really is colour blind. And mad. Even James May would think twice about buying an item of clothing that melded such inappropriate colours, and he normally looks like he gets dressed in the dark.

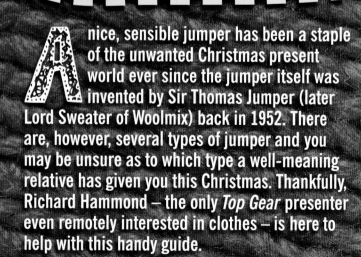

A nice, sensible jumper has been a staple of the unwanted Christmas present world ever since the jumper itself was invented by Sir Thomas Jumper (later Lord Sweater of Woolmix) back in 1952. There are, however, several types of jumper and you may be unsure as to which type a well-meaning relative has given you this Christmas. Thankfully, Richard Hammond – the only *Top Gear* presenter even remotely interested in clothes – is here to help with this handy guide.

THE EASY RETURN

The Easy Return can take many forms. The crucial part is the label which tells you it was bought from Marks & Spencer, because when you see this you know St Michael has reached down from on high and blessed you with the ability to take it back for a no-questions-asked refund or, if you haven't got the receipt, at the very least the chance to swap it for some socks. Result!

THE CHUNKY KNIT

Does your newly received jumper appear to have colour-coded mooring ropes stitched to the front of it? Are they so substantial that you could conceivably lose a pen and two apples between their hefty contours? Then you, my friend, have been given a chunky knit. Perhaps your grandmother mistakenly thinks you are a deep sea fisherman. Or Norwegian.

THE FESTIVE DESIGN

As you unfolded your new jumper from its wrapping, were you suddenly alarmed to see what appeared to be an eye? Did the eye then turn out to belong to an enormous Santa? Sounds like you've got a Festive Design jumper right there. And the thing about a jumper with a Santa or snowman or Christmas tree on the front is that you can wear it all year round. Oh no wait, you can't. Basically it works on one day of the year. For the other 364 days you'll look like a loony.

THE SLEEVELESS

Ah, now this is an easy one to spot. Has your new jumper got sleeves? If the answer is 'no' then you have one of these. The sleeveless jumper is ideal for someone who also enjoys a short-sleeved shirt. In other words, the kind of man who wears a massive watch and positions his Audi half an inch from your back bumper on the motorway.

GRANDMA'S HOMEMADE SPECIAL

The easiest way to identify this type of jumper is to ask yourself, was it given to me by my grandmother? And is your grandmother a knitting enthusiast? If you answer 'yes' to both of these questions then it's pretty certain that you've got a Grandma's Homemade Special on your hands. Other identifiers include a sort of rampant shapelessness brought on by not following the pattern, one arm significantly longer than the other, and the decision – brought on because you 'like pop music' – to embroider the front with foot high letters that spell out 'THE BEALTES'.

15 Crescent Road,
Grimblingham,
Hams,
GF5 6DS.

14 March 2011

MayTours,
Corduroy House,
Hammersmith,
London,
W6 8XY.

Dear Sir or Madam,

I wish to complain in the strongest possible terms about my recent experiences on MayTours' so-called 'Nurburgring Package' weekend break. I received this trip as a Christmas gift from my wife and, as a car enthusiast, I was extremely excited at the prospect of spending a couple of days at this hallowed and historic race track. You can therefore imagine my disappointment when the reality consistently failed to live up to the descriptions in the brochure.

For example, when it said 'Upon arrival in Germany you will receive a detailed briefing about the Nurburgring', I did not expect this to involve being locked in a hotel conference room with Mr May himself whilst he ranted about the 'ruination of the modern motor industry' for approximately seven hours.

The brochure also contained reassurance that if we had any questions during this briefing, Mr May would be 'happy to answer them'. Unfortunately, my question was 'When do we get to drive the Nurburgring?' to which he was happy to answer, 'Don't be a cocking idiot.'

However, the real insult came when we were led to what the brochure promised would be 'a range of interesting cars in keeping with the theme of the weekend'. I foolishly imagined these would be 'Ring-honed driving tools, such as the BMW M3 GTS and Nissan GT-R so you can imagine my crushing disappointment when we were instead confronted with a series of softly-sprung saloons including a Citroen C6, a Rover 75 and a 1979 Rolls-Royce Silver Shadow. Furthermore, although we were based at a hotel mere minutes from the Nurburgring, we were issued with a strictly prescribed driving route that almost wilfully took us away from the legendary track and suggested that if we wanted to stop at any point, the local castle was the 'only attraction in the area'.

Finally, the seemingly whimsical brochure slogan 'Dare you enter the gates of the Nurburgring?' took on an entirely more threatening aspect when it became clear that if we did attempt to drive through the gates, Mr May would leap out of a bush and attack us with a Taser gun until we turned around and proceeded back onto ordinary roads.

I would like to know what you intend to do about this highly misleading package tour. I would, however, advise you not to show this letter to Mr May himself since mere mention of the Nurburgring appears to make him deranged with anger and liable to deliver another insufferable monologue on ride quality.

Yours faithfully,

S. Smeeton

Simon Smeeton

STIG OVATIONS

FAST SOLUTIONS TO PROBLEMS YOU DON'T HAVE!

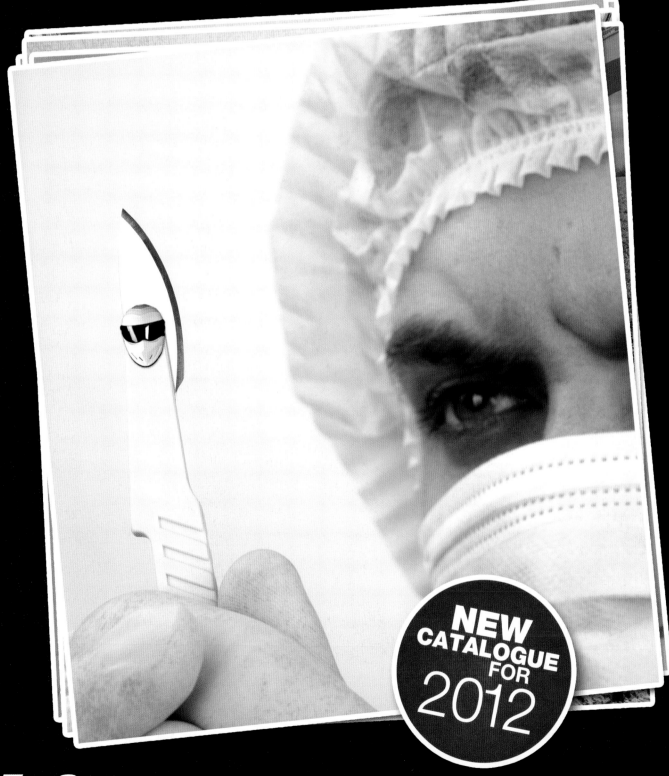

NEW CATALOGUE FOR 2012

TopGear

www.stigovations.com

GearStig

Change gear FAST with the shifting power of The Stig!

* ★ UNUSUALLY TEXTURED!
* ★ QUICK, QUIET GEARBOX OPERATION!
* ★ JUST £55!

ENHANCED GRIP FROM RUBBERY HELMET!

PrittStig

Stick things together FAST with the adhesive power of The Stig!

MYSTERIOUS, SILENT ★
STICKING POWER!
AUTHENTIC STIG SMELL! ★
JUST £2.50! ★

TO START GLUING PULL OFF HIS HELMET!

NIBBLE ON HIS HELMET!

Stiglets

Feed your hunger FAST with the snack power of The Stig!

* ★ CAN LAP YOUR INTESTINE IN RECORD TIME!
* ★ EXTREMELY YEASTY!
* ★ JUST £4.20!

Stwig

Hide male pattern baldness FAST with the concealing power of The Stig!

ACROSS THE (HAIR) LINE! ★
HIDES SLAPHEAD AND ★
IMPROVES AERODYNAMICS!
JUST £105! ★

MAKE YOUR HEAD LOOK LIKE HIS HELMET!

STAND BACK, HE'S GOT A HOT HELMET!

InStigerator

Dispose of industrial waste FAST with the firey power of The Stig

★ CAN INCINERATE LARGER OBJECTS INCLUDING TABLES AND CATTLE!
★ PLAYS RANDOM MUSIC!
★ JUST £435!

Heat-seeking misStigiles

Vanquish enemies FAST with the self-guided destructive power of The Stig!

★ MASSIVE BUT STRANGELY QUIET DESTRUCTION GUARANTEED!
★ TWICE AS POWERFUL AS DEL BOY TORPEDOES
★ JUST £9,999!

EXPLODING HELMET!

NIGELLA HAMMOND'S FESTIVE FEAST

Christmas lunch should be the most enjoyable meal of the year: Granny at the table! Dad carving the turkey! Paper hats and crackers! Sadly, the festive feast is also a minefield of culinary booby traps. But it doesn't have to be. The key to a successful Christmas day meal is PLANNING. And by using my easy-to-follow step-by-step guide, I guarantee your Yuletide gathering will be the talk of your street!

✶ THE DAY BEFORE – ASSEMBLING THE INGREDIENTS ✶

STARTER (Southerners only)

Many top chefs say that for the 'starter', you can't beat the traditional oak-smoked salmon, brown bread, butter and lemon. I say you can. I mean who wants to put their lives at risk with raw fish, from a river, that's been sat on some smouldering wood? And that's before you get to the merry hell of brown bread which almost certainly has bits in it. My alternative suggestion is to ditch it and get straight on to the main event...

MAIN COURSE

❊ THE TURKEY
There's a big fad for organic, outdoor-reared turkeys these days, but there's your problem right there: the word 'outdoor'. You just don't know where it's been. Play safe with a supermarket own-brand chopped and shaped Turkee™ joint. No muck, no guts, and it's been deep frozen for extra flavour.

❊ VEGETABLES
Sprouts, cabbage, carrots – all sorts of exotic Oriental produce makes an appearance at this time of year. I've even heard of RED cabbage, whatever that is! However, for this meal I'm a bit of a traditionalist, which is why I always plump for Bachelors Chip Shop Mushy Peas. Presentation is an oft overlooked skill in cooking, and in my Christmas meal, the bright green of the peas perfectly complements the white skin of the turkey.

❊ POTATOES
Yes.

❊ ACCOMPANIMENTS
There's lots on offer here and the shops can run you a right merry dance, so let me cut through the hype:
Stuffing – Can you really trust it?
Cranberry sauce – Sounds like a good idea, but unfortunately it contains cranberries, which are grown funny.
Sausages wrapped in bacon – Wrapping food in other food? No. Leave that gourmet stuff to Gordon Ramsay.
Gravy – That'd mean far too many flavours with the meat and peas. So no.
Bread sauce – Yes.

CHRISTMAS PUDDING

Two words: Mine field. The Christmas Pudding is basically a Trojan Horse for slipping all sorts of unwelcome ingredients onto the festive table, so be sure to take out everything you wouldn't want to eat:
Sultanas – This isn't Morocco.
Raisins – Not unless your family are rabbits.
Fruit peel – Pffft. We'll be eating potatoes in their skins next!
Suet – Yes!

❄ FOOD

As ever, planning is the key, so work backwards from when you plan to sit down. If it's, say, 2pm, then I recommend the following timetable:

1:00pm: Take Turkee™ joint out of freezer and pop it in oven on a very high temperature, as high as you like, really.

1:02 pm: Potatoes. Some people roast them in olive oil, rosemary and garlic. In other words, they ruin them. My method is simply to peel and place in boiling water.

1:10 pm: Open peas and pop on hob.

1:20pm: Mix suet with water, wrap in cloth and place in boiling water.

1:25 – 1:55pm: Baste turkey with fresh water, to prevent skin getting crispy.

2:00pm: Serve.

❄ DRINK

If ever there's a day to break out a bottle of wine, this is it. Here are my wine tips:

• Always check to make sure you've not picked up a bottle with a cork in the top. That's just making more work for yourself.

• Buy the best the corner shop has. It's Christmas!

• The French wines have really come on in the last few years, particularly ones from the Boardo region. I'd even venture to say they make a good alternative to English.

BOXING DAY TURKEY CURRY

Oh dear no. Far too spicy.

These and other recipes can be found on www.cuisinemidlands.co.uk

All I want for Christmas...

FIAT
PANDA

May 2004 to Apr 2011 (All Versions) Petrol & Diesel

Owners Workshop Manual

step-by-step maintenance and repair

Haynes
4889

4889

Extremely
Detailed
Edition

The best-selling car manuals in the world

THE VULCAN -
AN EXTREMELY
DETAILED
HISTORY

Christmas Geek

Impress your friends or get troublesome relatives to leave your house this Christmas by deploying these amazing car nerd facts.

The Jaguar CX-16 concept car is so named because it's the 16th Jag design project overseen by current styling boss Ian Callum.

The Lamborghini Aventador is named after a Spanish fighting bull of the 1990s who was famed for his exceptional spirit and bravery.

Following *Top Gear*'s short review of the Nissan Pixo, in which we basically said it was rubbish, UK sales of the car went up by 12 percent.

McLaren engraves its logo onto the crossmember behind the dash of the MP4-12C supercar rather than embosses it because doing so saves a few grammes in weight.

The tyre valves on the Bugatti Veyron Supersport experience such centrifugal force at high speed that they need a unique second spring to keep them shut, otherwise air would leak out.

There are no Porsches in the Forza 4 video game because a rival publisher holds the exclusive licence to put the German company's cars in games.

When Ferrari beheaded the 458 to create the Spider version, they re-tuned the exhaust so that it sounds at its best when the roof is off.

The Lexus LFA has a digital 'virtual' rev counter because its V10 engine revs too quickly for a normal analogue dial to keep up.

The retro looks of the new Mini and the Fiat 500 were overseen by the same man – Frank Stephenson. He's now in charge of design at McLaren.

The only real visual difference between the Range Rover Evoque and the LRX concept car that spawned it is a small air intake slot in the front bumper.

DO THEY KNOW IT'S STIGMAS?

It's Christmas time,
And the Yuletide season is here.
Christmas time
When we eat mince pies and drink warm beer.

Stuffed and warm and healthy
We're as happy as a manured-up pig
But listen Mister Wealthy –
Do you ever think of the Stig?

Oh, a Stig is for life not just for Christmas
And we've mistreated him for years,
Once he was full of innocence but now
He's the bitter Stig of tears.

Yes, there's a Stig outside your window
and a Stig who's cold and glum,
For underneath that helmet
Is a Stig who's duff's not plum,
And just because his jumpsuit
Is a snowman's snowy white,
Spare a thought for the Stigster
As he sleeps rough through the night.

Well, tonight thank God it's him instead of you!

And there won't be Stig in HMV this Christmas time
He won't be in Boots or Superdrug or Smiths
No Dixons vouchers for him
No presents, nor no gifts
Do you know it's Stigmas time at all?

Feed the Stig...
Feed the Stig...

(Repeat several times and fade)

SNOW?
JUST SAY NO

The boys' 'snowbine harvester' may not have been snapped up by councils looking to protect against another Arctic winter, but colder, snowier nations have come up with far bigger, more effective solutions for keeping their countries running when the snow and ice sets in. Here are a few of our favourites...

THE 1,400BHP SNOWPLOUGH

As Jeremy, James and Richard discovered, Norway has a lot of snow. Thankfully, the canny Norwegians have vehicles far better equipped than *TG*'s 'Dominator' at dispersing the evil white stuff. Like this monster, Overaasen's 1,400bhp snowplough that'll turn a nasty, slippery ski resort into a nice, snow-free, muddy hill in mere minutes.

THE V8 SNOWBLOWER

Trust the V8-obsessed Americans to build a snowblower around the nation's favourite engine. The perfect Christmas present for any safety-conscious father, this home snowblower packs a 7.4-litre, 400bhp Chevrolet V8 and is capable of clearing a ten-foot snowdrift from your front yard in seconds. WARNING: please make sure no pets or children are in the vicinity when operating your V8 snowblower.

THE RUSSIAN NUCLEAR ICEBREAKER

Capable of smashing through solid ice over 3 metres thick, Russia's latest generation of ice-breaking ships are powered by on-board nuclear reactors, some generating as much as 350 megawatts and sending over 200,000bhp to the ship's propellers. Used to forge routes through the frozen Arctic Circle, a nuclear icebreaker can spend up to four years at sea before needing to be refuelled, by which point its crew will have (a) beaten each other to death or (b) become very, very good at Scrabble.

THE ROTARY PLOUGH-TRAIN

Snow on train lines is bad news. Bad news that tends to end in derailing and crashiness. Though they've sadly been replaced in recent years by more modern, less lethal ploughs, the rotary snowplough is the undisputed daddy of the railtrack-clearing world. With dozens of chopping, slicing blades spinning at breakneck speed in front of a locomotive travelling at 50mph, the rotary plough can also be employed as an efficient-paper-shredder or cheese-grater.

One thing Mr Clarkson clearly wasn't joking about was his frequently expressed belief that his so-called 'sports train' was 'superb'. Sadly, in this regard he was mistaken, as we very rapidly learned when we climbed aboard and let the journey commence. Although it was a rather cold and miserable November day, it soon became apparent that the 'sports train' carriage lacked any form of heating, just as it also lacked any form of protection against wind, rain, flies and Mr Clarkson's attempts at 'catering' which revolved around throwing sandwiches and slices of cake at us from his (presumably relatively warm) position in the Jaguar's driving seat.

If coldness, wetness and being hit in the face with a Mr Kipling Fondant Fancy were the only problems with this journey, that would be bad enough. However, it is also worth noting that Mr Clarkson's train was both noisy and ridiculous, as was Mr Clarkson himself.

It was also desperately uncomfortable and, at speed, quite insanely frightening. In fact, it was a huge relief when – having almost collided with an enormous diesel locomotive and been forced to reverse two miles in the direction we had just come from – we eventually pulled into our final destination, an equally unromantic location best described as 'the outskirts of Peterborough'.

Unless your perfect romantic Christmas rail adventure involves abject terror, gross discomfort and getting covered in bits of wet food, we would strongly advise against this particular journey. ∎

and the excellent service leaves you refreshed and revitalised as the train pulls into Vienna, just in time for Christmas!

Finally, a sobering reminder that not everything billed as 'a festive getaway by rail' will deliver the romantic and relaxing experience you may be looking for. We sampled *I Promise You This Is Literally The Greatest Christmas Rail Journey Ever*, a curiously titled day trip from *Clarkson Tours* (www.lookatthisitismyinternet.tg) which utilises proprietor Jeremy Clarkson's unique 'sports train' to deliver an experience which is unforgettable for all the wrong reasons.

The package is billed as 'literally romantic' which seems strange because it began in a siding just outside Leicester. You may regard this as disappointing, unless your sense of romance is fuelled by drizzle and standing next to a ditch with an old training shoe it.

At just after the appointed hour, Mr Clarkson arrived driving an old Jaguar convertible which had been crudely converted to run on rails and was towing an old caravan which had the top half sliced off and four racing seats installed inside. Mr Clarkson's opening gambit was to shout 'Behold!' at us, shortly followed by 'Damn and blast!' as he realised he couldn't stop and slid inexorably past his four damp and depressed passengers. He later blamed this opening hiccup on 'the wrong sort of drizzle'. It is hard to know if Mr Clarkson was joking when he said this, just as it was hard to tell if he was joking when he later shouted, 'Something is usually on fire by now'.

> 66 If coldness, wetness and being hit in the face with a Mr Kipling Fondant Fancy were the only problems with this journey, that would be bad enough 99

DON'T WANT TO GET LOST
← THIS CHRISTMAS? →

THEN YOU NEED...

SANTA NAV

TV's Richard Hammond says...

"This Christmas getting lost will be no Claus for concern... Oh God, I just said that out loud"

TV's James May says...

"Don't worry, I had nothing to do with this"

TV's Jeremy Clarkson says...

"Literally six billion addresses. No really, for once I'm not exaggerating"

✱ Features every address in the entire world!
✱ Contains intricate details of roof camber and chimney access!
✱ Controls work even when fingers are covered in mince pie grease!
✱ Voice commands in English, Laplandish and Reindeer!

CHRISTMAS PRESENCE

Preparing to attend a Christmas party isn't just about dusting off those smart clothes and hoping to God you don't get stuck with that terrible man from Leeds who inexplicably calls you 'Roger'. It's also about making a good impression. In other words, you need to turn up in the right car with the right – ahem – Christmas presence, as shown in this handy *Top Gear* guide.

RANGE ROVER

They might have given it stupid twinkly lights and horrid shiny detailing, but the Range Rover still has a certain quiet majesty to it, which makes it the ideal way to fetch up at any Christmas event. And if any *Top Gear* presenters are there, they'll approve because it's one of the few cars that all three of them like.

ROLLS-ROYCE PHANTOM

Nothing gives everything a sense of occasion like the big Rolls which means you'll feel special, even if you're just going for a tepid mince pie at the house of some people you don't especially like. However, do be aware that sight of a Phantom might lead your hosts to assume that Simon Cowell is paying them a surprise visit and they will pretend to be out.

MASERATI QUATTROPORTE

Yes, it's a rather old design but it still looks sensational and it offers an effortless amount of elegance and charisma that will wow your hosts as you purr to a halt outside their house.
Either that or they will assume that Italian Prime Minister Silvio Berlusconi has turned up and will immediately hide their 18 year old daughter for fear that she gets a) whisked away in the Maserati and b) pregnant.

BENTLEY MULSANNE

Designed and engineered from scratch by Bentley's top boffins, the Mulsanne's styling is disappointingly square and boasts panel gaps so wide you could conceivably get into the car without first opening any of the doors. There's more disappointment with the engine which claims to be a 6.75-litre turbocharged V8 yet sounds like a knackered four cylinder from an old Fiat that is permanently on the verge of overheating. Despite the prestigious badge, frankly we wouldn't attend any Christmas event in this unless it was a banger race. Are we sure this is actually the new Bentley?

HUMMER H1

Ah, now here's a good example of how to get the Christmas presence thing wrong. The Hummer might be about the size of Shropshire and therefore quite hard to ignore but it creates wholly the wrong impression as it lumbers up to the party, largely by suggesting that you're the kind of person who will respond to the pulling of a cracker or the releasing of a party popper by firing a hand gun into the air. The H1 is simply too much.

MERCEDES CLK BLACK

Ah, now this really is too much.

WRAPPING PRESENTS

Step 1: Place the present on the wrapping paper to assess how much paper you will need to completely cover when opposing sides are folded so they meet in the centre of the item to be wrapped. Remember you will need less paper at the top and bottom of the item to be wrapped as these will be covered by folding in the ends of the paper in a four-way crossover.

Step 2: Once you have assessed how much paper you will need, take a pair of scissors and carefully cut out an even square or rectangle to the correct size.

Step 3: Place the present in the centre of the piece of paper and carefully fold both sides of the paper over so that they meet in the middle, slightly overlapping atop the present. Place a small piece of sticky tape in the centre of the paper to secure the two overlapping sides.

Step 4: With the present laying on a flat surface, take one end of the paper 'tube' that now surrounds the present and carefully fold the overhanging paper from the top so that it covers the end of the present. Repeat this technique for the flap of paper from the bottom. In doing so you will create two triangles of paper on the left and right hand side of the end of the present. Carefully fold these in to cover the end of the present and use a small amount of sticky tape to secure.

Step 5: Repeat the above technique for the other end of the wrapping.

Hey presto! Your friends and family will marvel at such a thoughfully wrapped gift!

This is all drivel

Here's the clarkson method...

① *Put the present literally on the paper.*

② *Literally tear around it.*

③ *Scrunch the paper literally around the present.*

④ *Literally put some tape on it.*

⑤ *Done. And it didn't literally take FIVE HOURS. JC*

The Top Gear Christmas Party

This exclusive photo, taken at last year's *Top Gear* seasonal bash, allows us to put names and faces to some of the people working behind the scenes on the world's favourite show that used to be about cars.

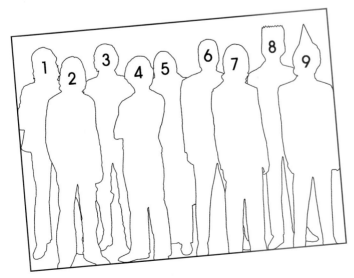

1. Nigel Glycerine
Deputy Director of Completely Spontaneous & Not Predictable Fires

2. Jonathan Literallee
Chief High Overlord of Exaggeration

3. Will Thatt-Islyke
Head of Metaphors

4. Cole Dandmiserabel
Director of Wearing a White Coat & Waving a Flag to Start a Drag Race

5. John Busihands
Audience Services – Pretty Girl Wrangler

6. Marc Malheureusement
Director of Safety

7. Ian Creasingly-Conttryved
Head Writer – *Stig Introductions*

8. Nicholas Strident
Director of Opinions

9. Mike Sporrts-Casuole
Head of Jackets

Not pictured –
Head of Foreign Relations

NEW RELEASES FROM
TG GAMES THIS CHRISTMAS

RICHARD HAMMOND'S ULTIMATE MORGAN RACING

A medium-paced battle of extremely old-fashioned sports cars! Line up on the grid, wait for the green light, then carefully take the old girl up through the gears before braking gently to pull over for a nice picnic! Realistic wooden chassis texturing and driver's idiotic hat rendering!

JAMES MAY'S GRAND THRIFT AUTO

You are TV's James May in a beige Volkswagen Jetta diesel! Keep your eye on the speedometer to maintain desirable levels of sensibleness! Slip gently into a coma!

JEREMY CLARKSON RALLY

You are a tall man in an ill-fitting race suit competing in a world class rallying event! Do not listen to your co-driver and just keep your foot down until you crash! Noisy and annoying!

ONLY AVAILABLE ON THE STIG STATION

TG GAMES

Preventing you from going outside and meeting people like a normal person

the Middle East

In *Top Gear*'s most ambitious Christmas road trip to date, our brave boys were given a challenge of literally Biblical proportions – to follow the path of the Three Wise Men across Iraq, Turkey, Syria, Jordan and Israel, all the way to the finish line in Bethlehem. Except the Three Wise Men never had to deal with landmines, food poisoning and scary border controls. They weren't driving three ageing roadsters either.

1. Aboard an old Russian transport plane piloted by an apparent lunatic. It's all going very well so far...

2. ...and now, to our boys' surprise, the old Russian transport plane is performing a scary landing in an even more scary place – Iraq. Gulp.

4. ...and find themselves cruising down an Iraqi dual carriageway, as you do. No problems so far...

3. Furnished with this new information about their landing point, our plucky lads decide to make a run for it...

5. ...except with James's BMW Z3, which has already broken down. As you might not expect, he HASN'T done things properly for once....

6. Our chaps realise Iraq isn't as dangerous as they thought. And it has some cracking roads through some beautiful scenery. Result.

7. 'Bulletproofing' the Clarkson way. In other words, 'badly'.

8. An Iraqi theme park. If you are standing here, your estimated queuing time is... erm... zero. Spooky.

9. Uh-oh, it's border crossing time. Hammond's novelty lighter suddenly doesn't seem so amusing. In fact, he almost soiled his pants. Although that might have been for other reasons. Foreign food really doesn't agree with him.

10. With Hammond confined to the lavatory, May and Clarkson put a CD on his Fiat's stereo – permanently. And it's the only thing in the world more horrible than food poisoning – prog rock.

11. Richard shares news of his bottom problems, little guessing that he's about to get a painful dose of Genesis.

12. Another problem – if our boys are spotted in Syria, that'll upset the Israelis and they won't be allowed into Bethlehem. There's only one solution...

13. ...and the solution is CAMOUFLAGE. Oh yes. Let the cross-desert sneaking commence.

14. Uh-oh. Whilst attempting to free a stuck car, May has fallen backwards and cracked his head on a rock.

15. 'Oh cork! No wait, that's not right. Where am I?'

16. He's okay! Although judging from the bandage, he might have been in a cartoon hospital.

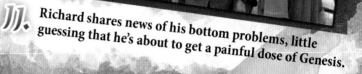

17. Our lads are doing something really brave. They're going deep into Jordan. Time for some Old Testament-style car racing at a handy hippodrome.

18. With Bethlehem getting closer, the boys hit the shops to find some gold, frankincense and myrrh. Or at least to find out what on earth they are.

19. Ah yes, that's gold. But then frankly that was the easy one. Frankincense? Myrrh? Do they even make that stuff anymore?

20. Oh dear. Our JC confuses himself with another chap who had those initials. Jeremy isn't really walking on water - he's just standing on a box.

21. And lo! A star (added in post production) guides our trio to a lowly stable...

22. ...and there a baby Stig was born. He's not the messiah, he's just a very quick driver.

Deck The Halls

Deck the halls with Jeremy Clarkson,
Fa la la la la, la la la la.
Though he can be enormously irksome,
Fa la la la la, la la la la.

Bring along his friend the Hammond,
Fa la la, la la la, la la la.
Fetch along some toast and jam and
We will watch them on TV,
Fa la la la la, la la la la.

See the blazing May before us,
Fa la la la la, la la la la.
Pray that he won't start to bore us,
Fa la la la la, la la la la.

Fast away the old year passes,
Fa la la la la, la la la la.
Let not our trio of themselves make asses,
Fa la la la la, la la la la.

For they might not ideal presenters be,
Fa la la la la, la la la la.
But there's still sod all on ITV,
Fa la la la la, la la la la.

CHRISTMAS FILM RECOMMENDATIONS

Christmas is fast approaching and that means plenty of great films on television. Here is our pick of the Christmas movies that might have particular appeal to electric car drivers like us!

PLUG ACTUALLY

(ITV2, 27 December, 9pm)

From British writer Richard Curtis, an amusing tale of eight very different couples, all experiencing the highs and lows of the same common theme – having only four miles range left and desperately trying to find somewhere to plug in their electric car before it completely conks out.

FLEX & THE CITY

(C4, 22 December, 10pm)

A horse-faced New York newspaper columnist and her three friends live a glamorous life of shopping, charging up their electric cars, dating, charging up their electric cars again, trendy restaurants, and trying to hail taxis because their electric car has run out of power and they're going to be late for some sex.

HARRY POTTER & THE PRISONER OF AZKABATTERIES

(BBC1, 26 December, 7pm)

In this, the third in the popular Harry Potter series, the young wizard encounters a man who is trapped by his car's inability to drive more than 100 miles without having to stop for a lengthy charging session. Sadly, even magic can't make his batteries fill up in less than 12 hours!

FIGHT PLUG

(Sky Movies 2, 26 December, 10pm)

Brad Pitt and Edward Norton star as two ordinary men whose lives are transformed after they become involved in a violent struggle to secure the last charging point in a supermarket car park.

LOCK, STOCK & TWO SMOKING BATTERIES

(E4, 22 December, 10:30pm)

Four Cockney geezers find themselves in debt to a local hard man and carry out a series of crimes in order to pay him back, all of which fail because their getaway car is electrically powered and runs low on charge after periods of hard acceleration.

and then lightly dust it with the remainder of the weasel cheese before dipping into the liquid nitrogen you prepared earlier.

49. Next, take the rest of the seagull and rub the iron filings into it before covering in the segments of Terry's Chocolate Orange. Place in the hessian sack along with the melon eighths and bear hands.

50. Telephone the actor and comedian Shane Richie. When he answers make a low-pitched rumbling sound and then hang up.

51. Take the pieces of magnesium you set aside earlier and throw them onto the pile of cats in the usual manner.

52. Cook some raspberry yoghurt under the grill and then pour over the rest of the potato carnage before sprinkling with feelings of despair.

53. Stare at a picture of a heron for 20–25 minutes.

54. Take a medium-sized hat and fill it with the lemons, ice cream, pork mince and cress. Smash.

55. Take the other half of the low mist and persuade it into the loose muesli. Add the spare hair and mix well using a system of pulleys and levers.

56. Omnislice.

57. Take the yeasty things out of the oven and slowly remove from their pan using a pair of heat-resistant trousers. Place them on a train to Ipswich.

58. Revolve slowly until filled with a sense of hope and nausea.

59. Remove the owls from their casket and add them to the main serving bag. Take care not to stain the other items.

60. Eighteen gallons of pear juice. Get rid of it.

61. Take your side gloves and garnish with wet bread, mousses and the remainder of the sleeves.

62. Remove your legs from the oven, drizzle with the after-dinner broccoli, add the wood peelings and gravel sauce, add to the plate with a slice of oxygen.

63. Throw directly into the sea.

Enjoy!

Q. Which family car is small, a bit daft and from Birmingham?

A. The Ford Hammondeo

Q. What's creamy, pedantic and goes well in a tuna sandwich?

A. James Mayonnaise

Q. Which Formula 1 driver is also a member of an orchestra?

A. Rubens Barri-cello

Which luxury saloon spends Christmas Eve delivering presents to children?

A. The Bentley Mulsanne-ta Claus

Q. Which American sports car can be used to make ratatouille?

A. The Chevrolet Courgette

Q. Which F1 pundit can lift 50 times his own bodyweight?

A. Eddie Jord-ant

Q. Which make of car is better shaken than stirred?

A. Aston Martini

Q. Which Czech car could be mistaken for a toadstool?

A. The Skoda Mushroomster

Q. What do you call a Japanese car that can be played by Parisian street musicians?

A. Honda Accord-ion

Q. What's tall, noisy and will give you a cold?

A. Germy Clarkson

Richard Hammond's
Believe It or Not!

THE WORLD'S LARGEST CAR IS A NISSAN MICRA SPECIALLY BUILT FOR STEPHEN FRY IN 1996. IT'S 1.5 METRES LONG AND 29 METRES HIGH.

DRIVING GLOVES WERE INVENTED BY SIR ALEC ISSIGONIS IN 1965 TO HIDE HIS HAIRY WEREWOLF HANDS.

BRANDS HATCH IS THE ONLY RACE TRACK IN THE WORLD THAT ALSO DOUBLES AS A GOLF COURSE, HENCE THE RECENT NEAR-DEATH OF JIMMY TARBUCK IN THE 2010 PRO CELEBRITY GRAND PRIX.

CHRISTMAS Pop Songs DISSECTED

1

I WISH IT COULD BE XMAS EVERY DAY
Wizzard

This is a Christmas classic, all right. It's got all the required elements – sleigh bells, a thumping great chorus, lashings of awful children, and it mentions snow and sleds and Santa with monotonous frequency. There's no doubt in the listener's mind that it's a Christmas song. Anyone mistaking this for a tribute to Lent has clearly been at the brandy. But the fellow singing it – Roy Wood – obviously has some issues. Number one: look at him. He looks like a burning clown. Number two: he can't spell Wizard. But number three is the most damning condemnation: what kind of moron wishes it could be Christmas every day? Most of us would be happier without Christmas every year. Christmas is an awful day full of relatives, expense and imminent constipation and yet Roy Wood seems to think we should have it on a kind of loop. He's like one of those Americans who has 500 Christmas lights on his porch and a big Santa that shouts 'HO HO HO' and runs up an enormous electricity bill so he has to go out and rob an ice cream parlour or similar. Nobody wants Christmas every day, not even Santa Claus. Especially not Santa Claus.

2

STEP INTO CHRISTMAS
Elton John

Christmas is a time for nostalgia. Remember how we used to go out carolling on Christmas Eve and then have a glass of punch before we returned to our wassailing? That's what Christmas songs should be. Proper songs! With a tune you can whistle and a lyric based on a tale from the Bible, preferably involving that nice Mr Jesus. But this? Apart from anything, it makes 'Christmas' sound like a sort of festive cowpat. 'I'm terribly sorry, Vicar, I appear to have stepped into Christmas.'

3

SIMPLY HAVING A WONDERFUL CHRISTMASTIME
Paul McCartney

This is just awful. And what's a 'Christmastime'?

4

DECEMBER WILL BE MAGIC AGAIN
Kate Bush

She's mad. And not just 'Kate Bush mad' either. Mad like a normal mad person. Since when has December been magic? It's the worst month of the year. It's cold and wet and everyone's going crazy trying to buy the last Stig in the shop and we're all amazingly stressed and the only relief is drinking yourself into a stupor. So no, December will not be magic and has never been magic. 'Tragic' maybe. Yes, if Kate Bush had written a song called 'December Will Be Tragic Again', she'd get our vote. Otherwise, put a cork in it Mrs Mad.

5

MISTLETOE AND WINE
Cliff Richard

Ah, a proper song with a message. And not just any message. A message from Sir Clifford of Richard. Christmas is a time for reflection, not just fun and partying. Oh, you can have your mistletoe and some wine, Cliff says, but there's also some 'Christian rhyme'. Not that 'rhyme' rhymes with 'wine', mind. Maybe it's Christian rhyme insofar as it's rhyme that asks you to forgive it for not being very good.

6

HAPPY CHRISTMAS WAR IS OVER
John Lennon & Yoko Ono

No, it isn't. If they'd called it 'Happy Christmas War Isn't Over' it would have been more accurate. Mind you, that would be the worst Christmas card ever. Nobody wants to get a Christmas card that says Happy Christmas War Isn't Over. Apart from possibly a general. Or someone who makes tanks.

7

LITTLE DRUMMER BOY/PEACE ON EARTH
Bing Crosby & David Bowie

What in the name of God possessed Bing Crosby – a perfectly decent old man with a nice hat – to go into the studio and make a record with a drug-addled cross-dressing glam-rock art pervert? Was Dean Martin unavailable? Were the Andrews Sisters visiting their mum? You can't actually hear David 'I am weird' Bowie taking drugs or seducing goats or whatever it is he likes to do, but it's almost certain that's what he's doing every time Bing is giving us his best 'a rap a pom pom.' And that's another thing – why is Bing doing the rap a pom poms and Bowie hogging the lion's share of the vocals? It's pop music gone mad.

8

SANTA BABY
Kylie Minogue

Good Lord! Will nobody think of the children! Although ironically, Dame Kylie is herself the size of a child and, as such, could easy disappear in a crowded playground if she wanted to hide during a chase.

9

MERRY CHRISTMAS EVERYONE
Shakin' Stevens

This is the kind of record Elvis Presley would have made in the 1980s. Not if he had lived, but if he was still dead.

10

MERRY CHRISTMAS EVERYBODY
Slade

Literally brilliant.

Iiiiiiiiit's Chriiiiiiiiist maaaaaaaaas!!

PALACE 'UNHAPPY' WITH WEDDING COVERAGE

Buckingham Palace has expressed its 'grave concerns' over the BBC coverage of the Royal Wedding which was masterminded by the team behind the popular motoring programme *Top Gear*. A palace spokesman said the Queen and other members of the Royal Family were 'extremely unhappy' with the live pictures from yesterday's event, most of which seemed to focus on the cars transporting the Duke and Duchess of Cambridge and their guests to Westminster Abbey and gave almost no air time to the couple themselves. Her Majesty is also said to be 'angered' by events that occurred during the marriage ceremony itself, notably the moment when Pippa Middleton's bottom exploded. ***Full story: page 3***

MAY OUT OF NEW GALLAGHER BAND

James May has been sacked as the keyboard player in Noel Gallagher's new band, just days after his new role was announced.

"It's his own fault," said the former Oasis star bluntly. "I told him to play my fookin' tunes but he just kept doing all that baroque shit". Sources say the final straw came during rehearsals at a West London studio when May abandoned his keyboards and was discovered in the yard outside, quietly dismantling the engine from a Triumph Spitfire.

NASA REJECTS TOP GEAR SHUTTLE PLAN

On the eve of the final flight of the Space Shuttle, *NASA* has turned down an offer from the presenters of the BBC's **Top Gear** programme to design and build a replacement for reusable space orbiter. The rejection follows a demonstration of the Top Gear Orbiter Prototype at Cape Canaveral in Florida, during which the Reliant Robin-based craft achieved an unsteady lift-off and then almost immediately crashed into the ground. Speaking shortly after the failed launch, James May, Top Gear Director of Space Programmes, expressed his disappointment at the incident. **"Oh cock"**, he said.

CLARKSON OLYMPIC CEREMONY BID FAILS

The organising committee for the 2012 Olympics has rejected a bid from Jeremy Clarkson to arrange the opening ceremony of the Games.

A spokesman for London 2012 said the Top Gear star's proposals were, **'at best unfeasible and at worst downright lethal'**. Clarkson's ideas for the ceremony included a fleet of power-sliding Jaguar XKRs, all of which were on fire, and a display of synchronised machine gunning designed to unsettle foreign athletes. The committee also turned down the TV presenter's suggestion that the Olympic flame be lit using **'a series of metal slides, a bucket of grease and a naked Amy Williams'**.

Top Gear in phone hacking scandal

The presenters of Top Gear have encountered a phone hacking scandal of their own this week, but not the sort you might imagine! Sources close to the popular show say that hosts Jeremy Clarkson and Richard Hammond **STOLE** a mobile phone from their co-presenter James May during filming on Tuesday and **HACKED** it to pieces with a **PICK AXE**. The successful **HACKING** was said to be an act of revenge after May prevented Clarkson from using a **FLAME THROWER** to 'organise' some library books.

NO WHO FOR TG'S HAMMOND

Top Gear's Richard Hammond will **NOT** be the next Doctor Who, according to BBC sources. The well-known presenter had been tipped to replace Matt Smith as the legendary timelord but insiders say the show's bosses found his clothes too unrealistic and saw no merit in a new direction for the character based around landing on distant planets and then moaning about how he didn't like the food.

THE NORTHPOLE POSITION

AN IGLOO
Leading down to Santa's Secret Factory, where *Top Gear* merchandise is made by happy workers. Yes, HAPPY. Got it?

A ROLLS ROYCE ON SKIS
Before you get too excited, the skis are a rather expensive optional extra.

SOME PENGUINS
Penguins generally live at the Antarctic, but these ones are on holiday.

ANOTHER IGLOO
A decoy igloo, in which The Stig keeps old helmets and his vast collection of old *'Allo 'Allo* episodes on VHS.

HELIPAD
For Russian oligarchs prepared to pay extra for a special something in their stockings.

SANTA'S FURNACE GROTTO
This is where all your letters and cards to Santa are burned after reading. The recycling people don't collect up here you see!

SANTA'S GLASS OF MILK WAREHOUSE
He keeps every single one. You don't really think he drinks the lot on Christmas Eve, do you? The man would be weeing off the end of his sled all night.

BI-POLAR BEARS
Sometimes they're happy, sometimes they're not.

ICEBERG
'Did you see me in *Titanic*? No, not that one. I was in the background...'.

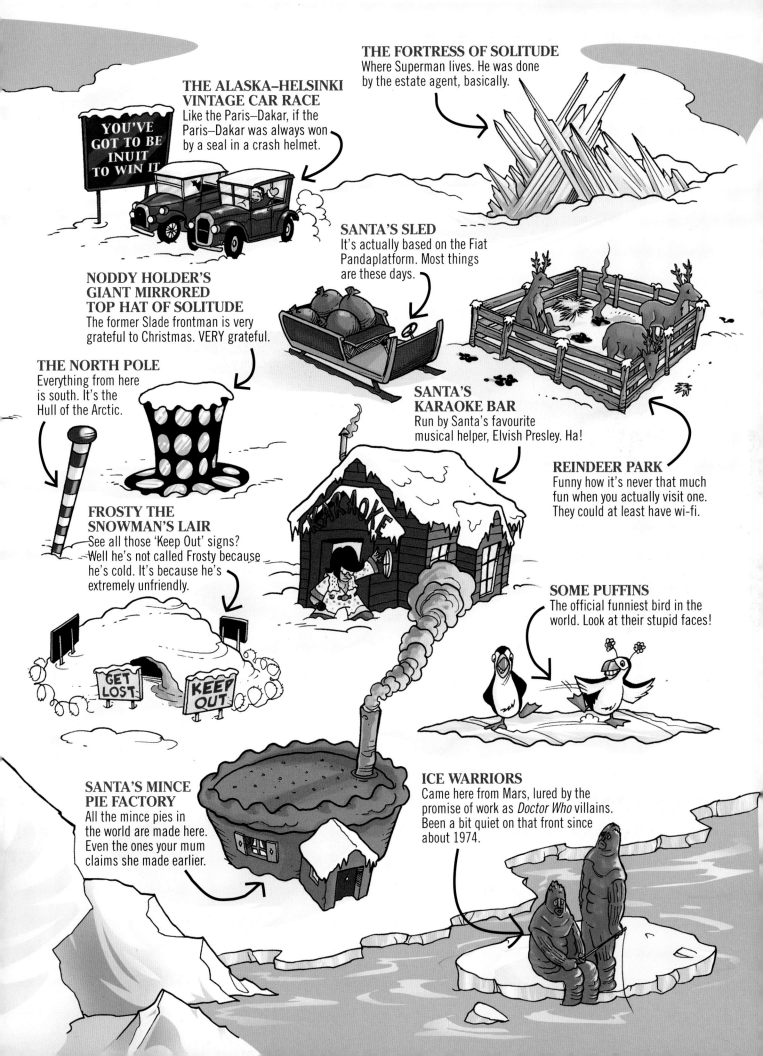

THE FORTRESS OF SOLITUDE
Where Superman lives. He was done by the estate agent, basically.

THE ALASKA–HELSINKI VINTAGE CAR RACE
Like the Paris–Dakar, if the Paris–Dakar was always won by a seal in a crash helmet.

YOU'VE GOT TO BE INUIT TO WIN IT

SANTA'S SLED
It's actually based on the Fiat Pandaplatform. Most things are these days.

NODDY HOLDER'S GIANT MIRRORED TOP HAT OF SOLITUDE
The former Slade frontman is very grateful to Christmas. VERY grateful.

THE NORTH POLE
Everything from here is south. It's the Hull of the Arctic.

SANTA'S KARAOKE BAR
Run by Santa's favourite musical helper, Elvish Presley. Ha!

REINDEER PARK
Funny how it's never that much fun when you actually visit one. They could at least have wi-fi.

FROSTY THE SNOWMAN'S LAIR
See all those 'Keep Out' signs? Well he's not called Frosty because he's cold. It's because he's extremely unfriendly.

KARAOKE

GET LOST

KEEP OUT

SOME PUFFINS
The official funniest bird in the world. Look at their stupid faces!

SANTA'S MINCE PIE FACTORY
All the mince pies in the world are made here. Even the ones your mum claims she made earlier.

ICE WARRIORS
Came here from Mars, lured by the promise of work as *Doctor Who* villains. Been a bit quiet on that front since about 1974.

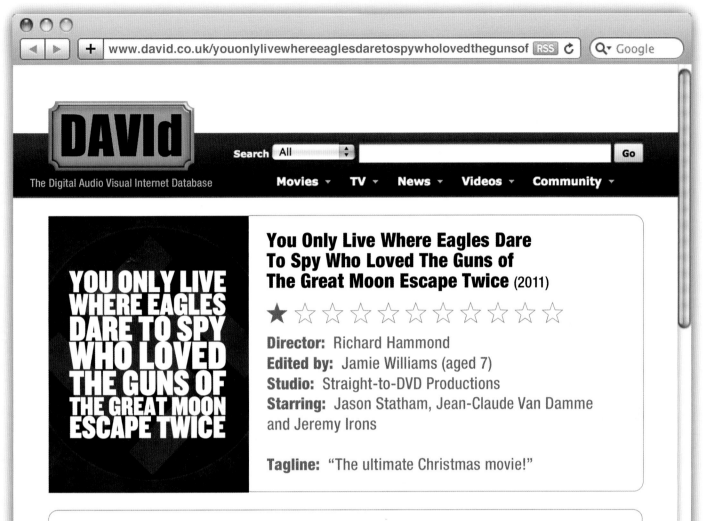

DAVId

The Digital Audio Visual Internet Database

Search All ▾ [   ] Go

Movies ▾   **TV** ▾   **News** ▾   **Videos** ▾   **Community** ▾

You Only Live Where Eagles Dare To Spy Who Loved The Guns of The Great Moon Escape Twice (2011)

★ ☆ ☆ ☆ ☆ ☆ ☆ ☆ ☆ ☆

Director: Richard Hammond
Edited by: Jamie Williams (aged 7)
Studio: Straight-to-DVD Productions
Starring: Jason Statham, Jean-Claude Van Damme and Jeremy Irons

Tagline: "The ultimate Christmas movie!"

Storyline:

It's 1943, the height of the Second World Cold War, and Secret Service Commando Tungsten Steel must stop SS Commie Nazi Colonel Fritz Stromfinger from using his diamond encrusted space laser to blow up the bridge over the guns of Navarone, an act which would cause the Soviets and the Americans to set off all their nuclear missiles. Having punched a Chinese man with metal teeth and a fez, Steel jumps his Aston Martin motorbike over a barbed wire fence and lands on the roof of a moving train where he has a fight with a shark, then steals the shark's jet pack and flies off the train just before it blows up and plunges into a ravine. Steel hovers down into a hollowed-out underwater volcano full of stolen submarines and a big clock counting down to zero. Just as the clock reaches 0:01, Steel manages to hack into the controls of the space laser and turns it on itself creating a massive explosion which allows all of his POW colleagues to escape down a tunnel whilst the blast blows Steel onto a cable car where he fights a man with an axe and then lands in the seat of a Lotus full of guns which he uses in a car chase with a load of KGB henchmen driving Hummers through the streets of San Francisco. The chase culminates with all the baddies driving onto the Golden Gate bridge which then blows up. In space.

Reviews:

"Complete drivel"
JONATHAN ROSS

"Confusing and unwatchable"
EMPIRE MAGAZINE

"Highly implausible"
JAMES MAY

"Not enough action"
JEREMY CLARKSON

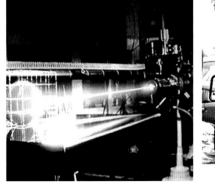

THE TEN MOST CHRISTMASSY CARS

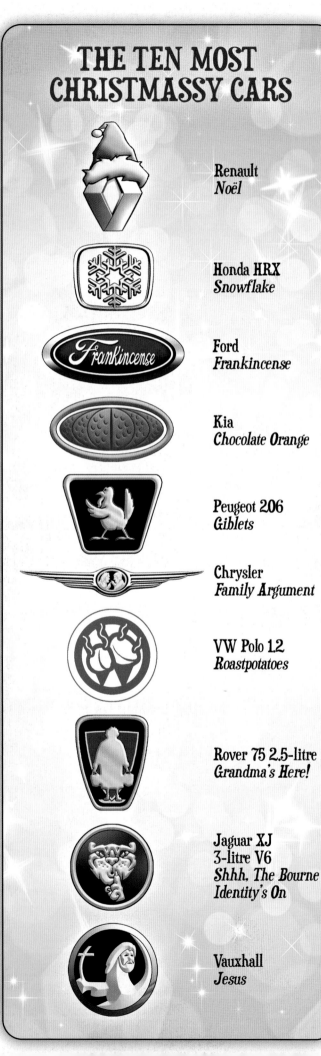

Renault
Noël

Honda HRX
Snowflake

Ford
Frankincense

Kia
Chocolate Orange

Peugeot 206
Giblets

Chrysler
Family Argument

VW Polo 1.2
Roastpotatoes

Rover 75 2.5-litre
Grandma's Here!

Jaguar XJ
3-litre V6
*Shhh, The Bourne
Identity's On*

Vauxhall
Jesus

RICHARD HAMMOND'S Believe It or Not!

'CAT'S EYES' AREN'T REALLY MADE FROM CAT'S EYES. THEY'RE MADE FROM THEIR KIDNEYS, BOILED UNTIL SHINY.

THE AUSTIN MAXI WAS THE FIRST CAR TO BE POWERED BY THE SHEER NOTION OF THE 1970S.

THE MOST FAMOUS CAR IN QUEBEC IS DEL BOY'S RELIANT ROBIN, WHICH WHICH HAS ITS OWN CHAT SHOW IN MONTREAL.

OBITUARIES

As is conventional at the turn of the year, *Top Gear* would like to pause and take a moment to mourn those brave souls who shuffled off the mortal coil in the last 12 months. Pray raise a glass to their tyre-shredding, petrol-gargling memories. Ashes to ashes, dust to dust, you had a good innings and now you shall rust...

Ford Focus RS

The most powerful front-drive production car in the world is dead, dead, dead. With its five-cylinder turbo making 300bhp – in fact, making 340bhp in final 'RS500' guise – the RS brought a whole new meaning to the phrases 'torque steer' and 'where did that tree come from?'. Ford has promised a new, yet-more-powerful RS will arrive some time in 2012, but it'll be a four-cylinder. Boo.

BMW M5

The V10-powered M5 was, since 2005, the car of choice for the discerning parent keen to get smoky and sideways with three kids and two spaniels on board. Sure, the

4.4-litre twin-turbo V8 of its successor may be more frugal and powerful – a full 52bhp more powerful, in fact – but it won't be as addictively raucous and rev-hungry. Pray bow your heads and mark the passing of the naturally aspirated M-car.

Audi RS6

Built for less than three years, the RS6's time with us was short but spectacular. Thanks to a pair of watermelon-sized turbos bolted to its 5.0-litre V10 engine, the four-wheel drive super-saloon produced a frankly unnecessary 572bhp and was capable of 0–62mph in four and a half seconds, and a top speed of 170mph flat-out. Even so, it wasn't capable of beating a pair of Unnecessarily Handsome French Skiers down a mountain. For bringing such shame on the automotive world, it deserved to die.

Mazda RX-8

Ladies and gentlemen, the Wankel is finished. Stop sniggering, you at the back. The RX-8's tiny, high-revving rotary engine can't be made clean enough to pass future emissions tests, so the strange-doored coupé has been unceremoniously killed off. However, Mazda has refused to give up on the venerable Wankel, hinting that a turbocharged version could feature in a future sports car.

Lamborghini Murcielago

Au revoir, you terrifying, lairy bastard. The bruising V12 Lambo has been laid to rest after nearly a decade in production, a run that culminated in the 690bhp, giant-winged SV – the car that, in the hands of Richard Hammond, ran the McLaren SLR 722 very, very close in a drag race across Abu Dhabi. Its replacement, the 691bhp Aventador, might be even quicker, but sadly has lost a little of the Murcielago's sofa-chewing lunacy.

Ferrari 612

Born in 2004, the 612 slipped away last year as quietly and meekly as it is possible for a giant V12 Ferrari to do. Yes, we shall shed a tiny tear for the 532bhp four-seater and its understated-yet-monstrous performance – 196mph, anyone? – but with the astonishing, 660bhp, four-wheel-drive, shooting brake Ferrari FF as compensation, we're struggling to miss it too much. Sorry, big guy.

Pagani Zonda

First introduced way back in 1999, when times were more innocent and global warming hadn't been invented, the Zonda is arguably the only modern supercar to truly muscle in to Ferrari and Lamborghini's playgrounds. The Zonda succeeded where so many others had failed for one simple reason: it was madder than a bag full of frogs, actresses and brushes. In final, definitely-not-road-legal 'R' guise, it produced 740bhp and was so noisy it clocked '14 Clarksons' on *TG*'s Decibelometer.

PEOPLE WE'RE NOT SENDING CHRISTMAS CARDS TO THIS YEAR

McLaren - not until they stop naming cars after photocopiers

Bentley - That car they left us in Albania was terrible

Audi — Won't stop putting twinkly bloody lights on everything

Aston Martin - The Cygnet. Dreadful

SAAB - Waste of a stamp?

Volkswagen - The new Beetle. Unforgivable.

Volvo - didnt build that sporty C30 Jeremy liked

Porsche - did build that diesel Panamera

Peugeot — usual reasons

MINI - the Countryman. Arrrrrgh, my eyes!

THE IN-CAR *TopGear* TEST

Simply attach the box to your dashboard and as you drive along you can enjoy specially recorded car review soundbites from Jeremy Clarkson, Richard Hammond or James May! Or combine all three and complete your journey listening to middle-aged men bickering!

Includes all your old favourite including, **'Poweeeeer!'**, **'That all sounds good, but... there's a problem'**, **'And it can also do this'** and **'It just works'**.

Jeremy Clarkson says, **'I promise you, this contains literally 10 million soundbites!'***

*WARNING: He might be exaggerating

THE PORSCHE GT3 RS KIT

MAKE YOUR ORDINARY CAR FEEL LIKE A TOP-OF-THE-RANGE RACING CAR FOR THE ROAD WITH THIS UNIQUE KIT INCLUDES:

◆ TOOLS TO REMOVE THE INTERIOR DOOR HANDLES AND REPLACE THEM WITH BITS OF FABRIC!
◆ GAUDY EXTERIOR STICKER KIT!
◆ PILE OF PAINT SCAFFOLDING TO COMPLETE REALISTIC INTERIOR 'ROLL CAGE'

THE MCLAREN *Joke* BOOK

Page after page of sensible, carefully optimised hilarity from the company that brought you the MP4-12C supercar. Includes such classics as,

'My dog's got no nose. How does he smell? Presently he doesn't due to the aforesaid lack of nose, however we have engaged in a research programme to construct a carbon fibre nose which will offer optimal olfactory performance combined with light weight and class-leading wetness'.

HADLEY'S ★ NEW ROMANTIC WAREHOUSE

Frilly cuffs! Strange waistcoats! Weird shiny jackets!

Hadley's New Romantic Warehouse lets you party like it's 1981! TV's Richard Hammond says, **'It's where I buy all my clothes!'**

JEREMY CLARKSON'S PATENTED CYCLIST DETERRENT

Simply attach the unique rotating blades to the side of your car and those impotently angry beardy bastards will never come near your car again!

The JAMES MAY VIDEO GAME STEERING WHEEL

Enhance your enjoyment of any popular driving game with this oversized Bakelite steering wheel, manual choke and full walnut dashboard!

Takes your virtual driving to a whole new level of ponderousness!

THE LAMBORGHINI CALCULATOR

Lamborghini has long been famed for its exciting supercars and seemingly sketchy grasp of numerical accuracy.

Now you too can enjoy some of that apparently plucked-from-the-air excellence with this unique calculator.

Simply enter a number and watch as it is magically rounded up to a different number that is larger than the one your competitor came up with!

Or engage the 'EU inspector is here' function to miraculously round down your figures so you won't get into trouble!

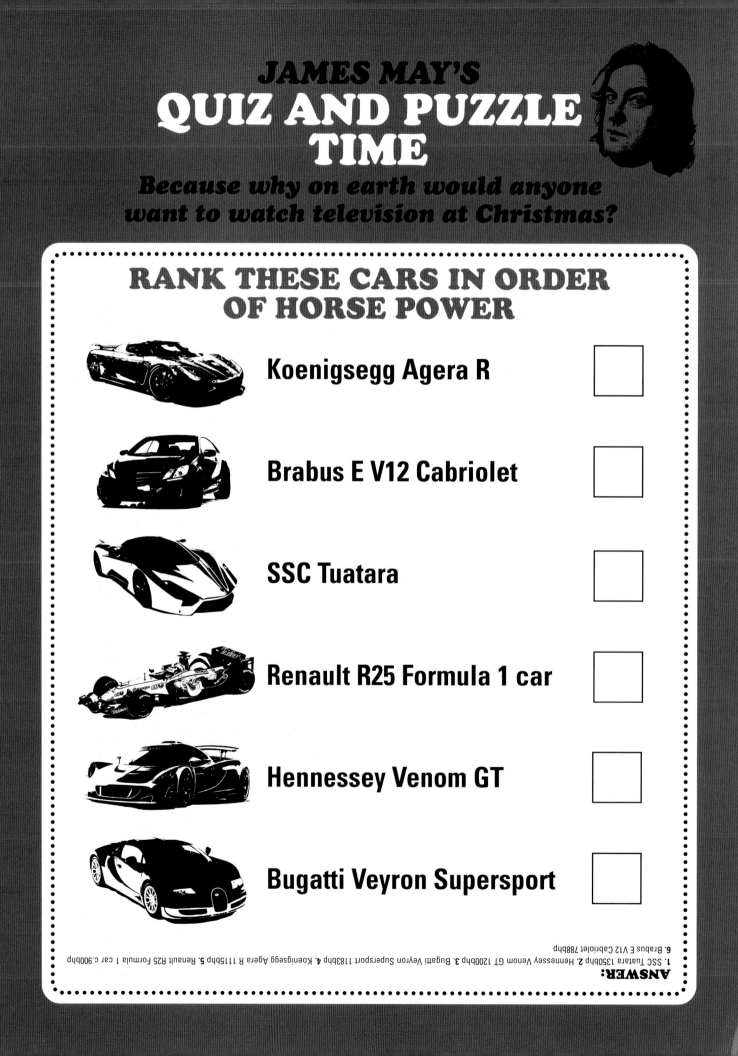

JAMES MAY'S
QUIZ AND PUZZLE TIME

Because why on earth would anyone want to watch television at Christmas?

RANK THESE CARS IN ORDER OF HORSE POWER

Koenigsegg Agera R

Brabus E V12 Cabriolet

SSC Tuatara

Renault R25 Formula 1 car

Hennessey Venom GT

Bugatti Veyron Supersport

BRITISH CAR WORD SEARCH
Find these hidden cars in the grid below

```
C O R N I C H E X U S L A S K E R T Y E I K F
Q K A N B S D E I P O E H G A E S P R I T I F
E N T U O R A P A C E P W Q I A K D H P L T R
S O E L J G A C E T L Y E W E N R O L P X N A
W B H R T O M C E P A T R E S S E F A D M M I
H L O F P O N C U T H E K I I M R L N H E O V
R E E A T P O I A W H F T E L N X D C H A T D
D E H N I M E T R O M E V P E Y E G H S P A R
I Y A E A N B R S T E M V S O R T K E W N R B
T H C I V J E A S L G T M O E B I O S X H N D
P D E R M A G N E T T E R H Q O L T T N A O O
Z A M P E T N I O N E Y W N A U S J E E N S L
X E S T I O M B F L A L V I S N E O R I Z L O
V A N T A G E J E E V X P L M W O A D E T Q M
P E R H I A M C H E Q A B D K A S C A R I L I
G R I F F I T H T R D B N K E S I O Y X N P T
A T S F O R M B A M X I L I E K X W U T R H E
S T A N K P O T E C H A P C Z I T P L O N S X
E N N A S L U M K L N E E A A P H F V M V L S
H E T O L P N V F A L I Y W R O M E S A K T E
D E F E N D E R O R N R R Y H A R C O I T M A
I U P O S G B E W E O S Z V E A U Y M F E P B
L O T S I R B N E N A X U Q S M A H R E T A C
```

PHANTOM	EVOQUE	RAPIDE
METRO	ATOM	MULSANNE
ETYPE	NOBLE	BRISTOL
CORNICHE	VANTAGE	CAPARO
ALVIS	ROVER	McLAREN
ELISE	DEFENDER	GRIFFITH
ESPRIT	CATERHAM	
LANCHESTER	DOLOMITE	
MAGNETTE	ASCARI	

ARE YOU A *TOP GEAR* ANORAK?
How much do you actually know about the TV show?
Let's find out...

1. During one of his 'thorough' car tests, Jeremy landed a helicopter on top of which car?

   ....

2. Who did Rowan Atkinson knock off the top of the Star in a Reasonably Priced Car leaderboard?

   ....

3. I raced British Winter Olympian Amy Williams in what make of rally car?

   ....

4. Which 1980s pop legend helped Jeremy's toppling Reliant Robin back onto its wheels?

   ....

5. What did Richard use as chase car for James's caravan airship?

   ....

6. On Clarkson and my electrically powered trip to the seaside, what make and model of car was I driving?

   ....

7. My sports motorhome was based on which car?

   ....

8. At the beginning of 2011, Richard achieved a childhood dream by driving a Ferrari F40 and which other car?

   ....

9. What was the original name of the presenters' Hammerhead Eagle iThrust electric car?

   ....

10. What make and model of sports car did I drive in the Middle East special?

    ....

11. Which American track did we visit with the Mercedes SLS, Ferrari 458 and Porsche 911 GT3 RS?

    ....

12. What was the exact model name of the BMW bought by Richard in the 'interesting cars for less than £6,995' challenge?

    ....

13. What was written down the side of Jeremy's 'sports train'?

    ....

14. In the *Top Gear* 'Ashes', Richard drove a transit van fitted with the engine from which supercar?

15. What is the fastest car ever to lap the *Top Gear* track?

16. What was the first car ever tested on 'new' *Top Gear* back in 2002?

17. What does The Stig's electric car-testing eco cousin have on the top of his crash helmet?

18. Who did Jeremy manage to fit into the boot of a Renaultsport Twingo?

19. As of the end of series 17 in July 2011, who is at the top of the F1 driver lap board?

20. What was the name of the steam train that Jeremy drove in the race from London to Edinburgh?

21. Richard based the Hammerhead Eagle i-Thrust on the chassis of which car?

22. Which current driver drove a 1988 McLaren F1 car during Jeremy's tribute to Ayrton Senna?

23. Who was the very first star in the Reasonably Priced Car?

24. Who wrote the original *Top Gear* theme tune and what is it called?

25. Which British Olympian's garden did the presenters 'improve' in the Sport Relief *Top Ground Gear* Force special?

Delight a friend, relative or fellow prisoner this Christmas with a book by their favourite Top Gear Presenter!

Literally Everything Is Annoying and Doesn't Work

by Jeremy Clarkson

A brand new collection which brings together some of Clarkson's most curmudgeonly and disgruntled rantings, including the legendary 'What is the point of nail scissors', the classic 'All clouds are fat idiots', and the famous 'I can't find my car keys and it's all the fault of Ed Balls'. Contains a particularly amusing final chapter in which Jeremy spends 750 words complaining about the tall man who's constantly on his landing moaning about things before remembering that someone in his house has installed a new floor-length mirror.

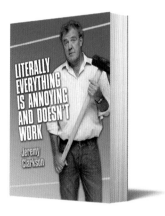

The Brummie Cookbook

by Richard Hammond

A wonderful new compendium of unimaginative and flavourless recipes, personally compiled by a man from the Midlands who doesn't like food with bits in it. Highlights include 'plate of beans', 'soup in a mug' and a spaghetti bolognaise with just three ingredients, one of which is spaghetti. Also contains recipes aimed at anyone who wants to make 'curry, but not that spicy stuff' and a lengthy section entitled 'Ordering a take away pizza and making sure they don't put any fancy nonsense on it'.

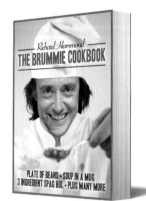

How Screwdrivers Work

by James May

You might think it impossible to write an entire 450-page book about the workings of an extremely simple device with no moving parts. But that's because you reckoned without the minutiae-based mind and pedantic power of James May. Although in fairness, this book isn't entirely about screwdrivers. There's a bit of an unintended deviation into the workings of air-traffic control that lasts from chapters 9 to 13, and most of chapter 24 is taken up with a lengthy ramble about why making a cup of tea should always be done with your trousers on.

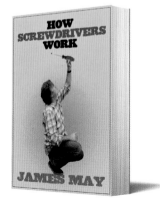

TROUBLESHOOTING GUIDE

If you are having problems with this book, please consult this table.

SYMPTOMS	SOLUTION
Book seems only half as wide as it should be. Also, there aren't many things to read.	Check that book has not been closed.
Book feels warm and cheesy. Also, has pepperoni and jalapeno peppers on it.	Check you are not reading an American hot pizza.
Book looks like a horrible cartoon car and makes everyone vomit.	Check book has not been swapped for a Mini Countryman.
Book is quite hairy and makes heavy breathing noise.	Check that you are not erroneously holding a dog.
Book is a load of whimsical nonsense about a tough boss who tries to marry her male assistant and it appears to have Sandra Bullock in it.	Check your copy of *A Top Gear Christmas* has not been swapped for a DVD of *The Proposal* starring Sandra Bullock.
Book appears to be entirely devoted to house prices, immigrants, and Princess Diana.	Check book has not been swapped for copy of the *Daily Mail*.

ERRATA

P21 – Since this page was printed The Stig has been removed from the periodic table.

P37 – Jeremy Clarkson is not, as stated, the High Overlord of Ipswich.

P42 – Michael Winner did NOT attempt to eat a shire horse.

P47 – Caption should read, 'the second row of a *Top Gear* audience' and not, as stated, 'A mound of Subaru branded rally polo shirts and caps'.

P64 – Photograph depicts the model and author Jordan and not, as stated, 'utter awfulness'.

P70 – The Richard Hammond Trouser Museum has since closed.

P86 – This page is wrongly labelled as safe to eat. The edible page is 94.

P88 – This really shouldn't be here at all.

P97 – Third paragraph might mistakenly imply that James May lives on an oil rig.

P101 – Picture on bottom right should be captioned 'The Vauxhall Oesophagus'.

P114 – There is absolutely no suggestion that this really happened, nor that the television journalist Andrew Marr was there at the time.

P121 – This page really should not smell like this.

INDEX

10 9 8 7 6 5 4 3 2 1

Published in 2011 by BBC Books, an imprint of Ebury Publishing, A Random House Group Company

The Random House Group Limited Reg. No. 954009 Addresses for companies within the Random House Group can be found at www.randomhouse.co.uk

A CIP catalogue record for this book is available from the British Library.

ISBN 978 1 84 990154 3

The Random House Group Limited makes every effort to ensure that the papers used in our books are made from trees that have been legally sourced from well managed and credibly certified forests. Our paper procurement policy can be found on www.randomhouse.co.uk

Written by Richard Porter & David Quantick with Andy Wilman and Sam Philip

Commissioning Editor: Lorna Russell
Cover Art Direction: Charlie Turner
Project Editor: Caroline McArthur
Design: Media Junction –
www.mediajunction.co.uk

Printed and bound in Germany by Mohn Media GmbH

BBC Books, Top Gear and the authors would like to thank the following for their help in creating A Top Gear Christmas:
Jeremy Clarkson, Richard Hammond and James May.
Nick Dalton, Tom Ford, Greg Vince, Adam Waddell, Julianna Porter, Anthony Williams, Adam Robinson, Nick Linford, Alex Hobbs, Rye Rahman, Jon Stephenson and the team at Media Junction.

Picture credits:
BBC Books and Top Gear would like to thank the following for their help in sourcing and providing photographs and for permission to reproduce copyright material.
While every effort has been made to trace and acknowledge all copyright holders, we would like to apologize should there be any errors or emissions.

BBC and BBC Worldwide Ltd. for all images apart from the following:

Front cover illustration by Engine Creative – www.enginecreative.co.uk

Illustrations pp. 4, 9–9, 19 b, 20–23, 31, 32–25, 42–3, 52–3, 65–71, 84, 90–1,102 t, 104–5, 114 by The Comic Stripper © BBC Worldwide

All created artworks © Media Junction unless otherwise stated; 28 t © Pagani, m © Porsche, b © Audi; 29 t © Alfa Romeo, m photographed by Ripley & Ripley for Top Gear Magazine, b © Toyota; 44 t © François Dorothé, m © Getty; 45 1 © Alamy, 2 © Tuatara, 3 © Alamy; 59: bm Alamy; 60 m © Motoring Picture Library, b © Corbis; 61 1 © Ian Seabrook, 2 © Motoring Picture Library, 3 © Alamy; 80 © BROOKE WEBB/Rex Features; 85: tl Alamy; all except tl Getty; 86 t & 87 t © Corbis; 90 t © Range Rover, m & b Alamy; 91 m © Getty; 93 © Advertising Archives; 101: 3 & 4 © Olga Besnard / Shutterstock.com; 103: © Stacy Morrison/Corbis; 106 t Alamy; 115 tl © Ford Motor Company, m © BMW, b © Audi, rt © Mazda, rtm © Lamborghini, mbr © Ferrari, br © Alamy. All other images supplied by shutterstock.com.